A New Library of the Supernatural
the Supernatural

Ghosts and Poltergeists

Ghosts and Poltergeists

by Frank Smyth

Doubleday and Company, Inc. Garden City, New York, 1976

EDITORIAL CONSULTANTS:

COLIN WILSON
DR. CHRISTOPHER EVANS

Series Coordinator: John Mason
Design Director: Günter Radtke
Picture Editor: Peter Cook
Editor: Eleanor Van Zandt
Copy Editor: Mitzi Bales
Research: Frances Vargo
General Consultant: Beppie Harrison

Library of Congress Cataloging in Publication Data
Smyth, Frank
Ghosts and Poltergeists
(A New Library of the Supernatural; v.8)
1. Ghosts 2. Poltergeists I. Title II. Series
BF1461.S63 133.1 75-26143
ISBN 0-385-11315-3

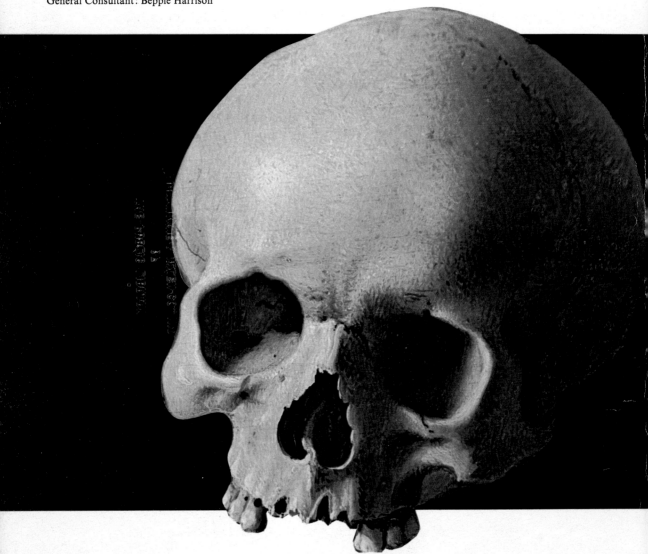

Doubleday and Company
ISBN: 0-385-11315-3

Library of Congress Catalog
Card No. 75-26143

A New Library of the Supernatural
ISBN: 11327-7

© 1976 Aldus Books Limited, London

Printed and bound in Italy by
Amilcare Pizzi S.p.A.
Cinisello Balsamo (Milano)

**Frontispiece: French painting of a ghostly gathering.
Above: are bones all that remain of the dead?**

Ghosts and Poltergeists

Is there really "no such thing" as a ghost, as the skeptics claim? Serious research on the subject suggests strongly that ghosts do exist — but exactly what they are remains a mystery. This book examines, through personal experiences and scientific studies, some answers to this fascinating question.

Contents

1

Seeing and Believing

As a young man living in Boston, the writer Nathaniel Hawthorne often used to go to the Atheneum Library. Among the distinguished men he usually saw in its reading room was the Reverend Doctor Harris, a clergyman in his 80s, who could be found every day about noon sitting in a chair by the fireplace reading the *Boston Post*. One evening, having visited the Atheneum that day and having remembered seeing Dr. Harris sitting in his chair as usual, Hawthorne was astonished when a friend told him that the old man had recently died. He was even more astonished when, on entering the reading room the following day, he again saw Dr. Harris reading his paper by

Above: this figure placed outside an amusement park "spook house" represents the popular notion of ghosts as mythical scary creatures no one really believes in.

Right: a real ghost? This photograph was taken in 1959 in the Australian bush by Reverend R. S. Blance. Although the site had once been used by aborigines for gruelling initiation ceremonies, it was deserted except for the photographer when he took this picture. Technical examination of the film ruled out double exposure. Photographs of apparitions (or seeming apparitions) are very rare, but they provide one piece of evidence supporting the argument that ghosts exist.

"What are we to make of this story?"

Below: the American novelist and short story writer Nathaniel Hawthorne. The author of many stories dealing with the supernatural, Hawthorne had several encounters with real-life ghosts. The house he lived in in Massachusetts was haunted, but the apparition confined itself to the front yard. "I have often," wrote Hawthorne, "while sitting in the parlor, in the daytime, had a perception that somebody was passing the windows—but, on looking toward them, nobody is there." The ghost Hawthorne saw in the Atheneum Library, however, was less elusive. In fact it sat in the same place for weeks, reading a newspaper.

the fire. Hawthorne spent some time in the room, reading and occasionally stealing a glance at the seemingly solid, lifelike apparition. For weeks he continued to see the old man in his chair. "At length," reported Hawthorne, "I regarded the venerable defunct no more than the other old fogies who basked before the fire and dozed over the newspapers." None of these living "old fogies" seemed to see the ghost although many of them had been close friends of Dr. Harris. So it was the more odd that his ghost appeared to Hawthorne, who knew him only by sight. Perhaps, however, the others did see it, but were as reticent as Hawthorne about acknowledging it.

Describing the incident years later in a letter to a friend, Hawthorne marveled at his own reluctance to investigate the phenomenon—to brush against it or try to snatch the paper, if it was a paper—out of its hands. "Perhaps," he said, "I was loth to destroy the illusion, and to rob myself of so good a ghost story, which might probably have been explained in some very commonplace way." In time, Hawthorne said, he became aware that the old gentleman seemed to be gazing at him with a certain expectancy. The novelist thought that maybe he had something to communicate, and was waiting for Hawthorne to speak first. "But, if so, the ghost had shown the bad judgment common among the spiritual brotherhood, both as regarded the place of interview and the person whom he had selected as the recipient of his communications. In the reading room of the Atheneum, conversation is strictly forbidden, and I couldn't have addressed the apparition without drawing the instant notice and indignant frowns of the slumberous old gentlemen around me. . . . And what an absurd figure should I have made, solemnly . . . addressing what must have appeared in the eyes of all the rest of the company, an empty chair. Besides," concluded Hawthorne, in a last appeal to the social proprieties, "I had never been introduced to Doctor Harris. . . ."

One day the figure was missing from the chair by the fire, and Hawthorne never saw it again.

What are we to make of this story? Was Hawthorne the writer simply spinning a yarn? Probably not, for as a skilled literary craftsman, he would surely have constructed his fictional ghost story so that it had some development and point. As fiction, the story is a bit flat. As a psychic experience, however, it is first class. This is no vaporous and transparent "gray lady" glimpsed for a few seconds in a darkened hallway by an impressionable person with weak eyesight. Instead, we have an apparently solid figure seen continually over a period of weeks by a man who—although sensitive and attracted to the mystical—was obviously clear-headed. What did he see?

Many people would have had a ready answer: Hawthorne saw the spirit of the deceased Dr. Harris, which for some reason was delayed in its progress into the next world and was temporarily trapped in the place he had "haunted" while alive.

The belief in an afterlife, held by almost all peoples since earliest times, once gave ghosts a legitimacy they lack in our more skeptical culture. Most religions have assumed the existence of a place, or places, where departed spirits go, and have provided rites to ensure the soul's passage into the next

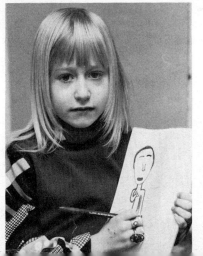

Above: in the mid-19th century the new art of photography joined with the new cult of Spiritualism to produce pictures such as this ingenious fabrication. The despondent widower, presumably lost in reminiscences, is visited by the ghost of his beloved wife.

Left: eight-year-old Beverley Dennis of Birmingham, England, holds a picture she's drawn of "Old Albert," an apparition that haunts her home. "He's an old fat man with a walking stick," says Beverley. "He has never hurt me, but I am frightened." Neither of her parents has seen the ghost, but they have been alarmed by frequent mysterious noises and movement of objects in the house, and have applied to the local public housing agency for a different house. Neighbors say that Beverley's description of the ghost (if not the slimmed-down drawing) fits a previous tenant named Albert.

9

world. Still, in varying degrees, people have believed that there was a certain connection between body and spirit, even after death, and that it was most important to bury the body in such a way that the spirit of the deceased would not come back to haunt the living. Some primitive peoples, for example, bind the arms and legs of the corpse to prevent perambulation after death. Traditionally, people have believed that if the person died without receiving the rites, and especially if he died by his own hand or in other violent or tragic circumstances, his spirit might remain earthbound.

One such imprisoned spirit was the object of the first recorded case of psychical research. In Athens, in the 1st century B.C., there was a house reputed to be haunted by a specter of a gray-haired old man whose hands and feet were bound in iron chains—a style of ghost later immortalized as the chain-rattling Marley in Dickens' *A Christmas Carol*. This ghost was said to have frightened one man to death, and in time the house fell vacant. Eventually the owner of the house, desperate to get some return from his property, reduced the rent to a ridiculously low figure. Hearing of these bargain-rate premises, the philosopher Athenodorus made inquiries, and was intrigued to learn the reason. He promptly moved in to investigate, and on the first night was rewarded by the sound of rattling chains.

In a moment the thin gray figure of the manacled specter appeared in the room and beckoned to him. Athenodorus ignored it. The ghost moved closer, clanking and rattling in agitation and beckoning all the while. Still the philosopher remained motionless. Finally the ghost gave up the effort, turned, and dragged its fetters out into the courtyard where it suddenly vanished. Out of the corner of his eye Athenodorus watched it go, and carefully noted where it had disappeared.

The following morning he went out, got a magistrate, and returned to the courtyard. After some digging they discovered a chained skeleton, its bonds covered with rust. The magistrate arranged for it to be given a decent burial, and the ghost was never seen again.

About 2000 years later a similar case of apparent cause-effect haunting came to light in England. Eric Maple, a folklorist and collector of ghostly lore, was interviewing some people in the village of Reculver, Essex, the site of a Roman settlement. The villagers told him about a clump of trees nearby that was haunted by the spirits of some babies, whose piteous crying disturbed the winter nights. Several of Maple's informants swore that they had heard these doleful sounds, and that on no account would they go near the "children's wood."

In the 1960s a major archeological excavation took place in Reculver during which a number of important Roman remains were unearthed. Eric Maple visited the dig in time to see a collection of children's skulls and bones discovered by the excavators. Analysis of the bones showed them to be at least 1500 years old. They included one complete skeleton of a child who had apparently been ritually murdered and interred in the foundations by the Gaulish soldiers encamped there. Here was evidence that the grisly custom of making a foundation sacrifice to the gods, common in many parts of pre-Christian

Ghosts are found in the folklore, art, and literature of all nations. Above: a typical Japanese ghost with flowing white gown and dishevelled hair, bending over a terrified mortal. Japanese ghosts are often shown without legs, and ghosts of people who led a wicked life are often physically deformed to suggest punishment after death. In Japanese folklore ghosts often visit people to warn them of approaching death. One writer, Inouye, remarks that "they are especially likely to be seen by persons who are out of health or . . . feeble in body and mind, deficient in knowledge and impressionable."

Right: this gargoyle on the Cathedral of Notre Dame, Paris, is a typical medieval representation of a demon, placed on a church to guard it from other demons. The Church believed that demons could assume the form of ghosts.

Left: the entrance to an amusement park "spook house" showing the kinds of terrors offered inside. People love to be frightened by make-believe versions of the supernatural, such as ghost stories and vividly hideous papier mâché specters that pop out of the dark. Yet most of the well-authenticated accounts of seeing a ghost involve no horror. Usually, the percipient is not even frightened. Many apparitions are so lifelike that they are mistaken for humans.

11

Above: in Shakespeare's famous play, Banquo's ghost appears to the terrified MacBeth, who has had Banquo murdered. He cries out to the apparition—which he alone can see—while Lady MacBeth assures the guests that her husband is merely suffering a momentary fit.

Below: the specter of the murdered Duke of Gloucester, in *Henry IV Part 2*, appears to his murderer, the dying Cardinal Beaufort.

Europe, had been done surreptitiously after the practice had been officially condemned. The question is: did the discovery of the bones at Reculver give substance to the phenomenon of the crying in the wood, or had the ancient story of the murder created the idea of children crying in the wood?

Pre-Christian Europe was thickly populated with ghosts, spirits, fairies, gods, and goddesses. Christian missionaries tried to discourage the native belief in such beings, but ended by absorbing some of them in altered form into Christian teaching. The grotesque gargoyles that perch on the roofs and towers of some medieval churches are evidence of the survival of the pagan superstition that a demon could be used to frighten away other demons. This belief was adapted to protect the Christian faithful inside the church.

Ghosts were looked upon with some suspicion by the Church. It was generally assumed that a demon who was unable to find a weak-willed human to possess might create a visible form for himself and appear as a ghost. The Church allowed that some phantoms were those of souls in Purgatory, and that a very few might be saints, but warned its members to treat any specter with caution.

This wary attitude toward ghosts is one of the elements in the plot of *Hamlet*. When he first sees the ghost of his murdered father, Hamlet acknowledges the possibilities of its being evil: "Be thou a spirit of health, or goblin damn'd, / Bring with thee airs from heaven, or blasts from hell, / Be thy intents wicked or charitable, / Thou com'st in such a questionable shape, / That

I will speak to thee. . . ." Later, although almost entirely convinced of the truth of the ghost's claim that his own brother murdered him, Hamlet hesitates to avenge the murder, partly because he has a nagging doubt as to the ghost's true identity. "The spirit that I have seen / May be a devil, and the devil hath power / To assume a pleasing shape." He arranges a play depicting a similar murder, hoping to trick the king into revealing his guilt and thereby verifying the ghost's accusation.

Interestingly the *Hamlet* ghost is not visible to everyone—just as Hawthorne's ghost was not. Hamlet's friends see it, but his mother does not. When the ghost appears in the queen's room and Hamlet speaks to it, he alarms the queen who sees nothing. Already suspecting that her son is mad, she tells him: "This is the very coinage of your brain."

The queen's interpretation of Hamlet's ghost is the skeptic's interpretation of all ghosts. An apparition—and to the skeptical this word is much preferable to ghost, which implies a surviving personality—is simply a picture conjured up by the person who sees it. Determined scoffers are inclined to believe that anyone who sees a ghost is, at least temporarily, mentally unbalanced. More objective researchers will tend to agree that a ghost is indeed a kind of picture, but that it may not necessarily originate in the brain of the person who sees it. The wealth of evidence accumulated on apparitions and hauntings so far contains many questions that cannot be answered by any one theory.

Even the most thorough skeptics will usually show a reluctance to confront specters, imaginary though they believe them to be. In an introduction to a collection of ghost stories, Bennett Cerf pokes gentle fun at "the greatest skeptic I ever met [who] was asked point-blank if he would sleep alone in a house that had been haunted, according to common belief, for a hundred years or more. 'Not on your life!' said the skeptic. *'Why should I take the chance?'*"

The potentially frightening aspect of ghosts is one reason for their enduring popularity in legend and literature. The psychical researcher may be more interested in cases that have an aura of prosaic normality about them, such as Hawthorne's; but the average person is more likely to be intrigued by ghosts that terrify. Ghostly lore abounds with phantoms that have empty eye sockets instead of eyes, or are missing their heads, or are skeletons. According to a legend of Norfolk, England, every May 31 at midnight a phantom coach that sets out from the village of Bastwick is driven furiously through the countryside by a mad coachman. The coach appears to be on fire, but the sharp-eyed or imaginative observer may catch a glimpse of its passengers—who are skeletons. Eventually the coach crashes into a bridge and the whole thing, including horses, driver, and occupants, plunges into the water. As the story goes, this ghastly conveyance recalls the marriage in 1741 of Sir Godfrey Haslitt of Bastwick Place, and Evelyn, Lady Montefiore Carew of Castle Lynn, a match arranged by the bride's mother with some help from the Devil. The marriage festivities were barely over when the Devil claimed his own—not only the ruthless mother, but also the bride and groom, all of whom lost their lives in a fire that burned down Bastwick Hall.

Below: a scene from one of the best-loved of all ghost stories, Dickens' *A Christmas Carol*. **Here the miser Ebenezer Scrooge is visited by the ghost of his former business partner Jacob Marley. Moaning in anguish for his ill-spent life and present torment, Marley warns Scrooge that he too will be condemned to an afterlife of suffering unless he mends his ways and learns charity toward his fellow men.**

Life in Death

In 1878 the daughter of D. J. Demarest, a grocer of Paterson, New Jersey, died apparently of a heart disease. The child died on a Tuesday, and the body was dressed for burial and laid in its small coffin. On Friday, the father left the coffin where he had been kneeling, and went into the next room. There he sank into an armchair, hid his face in his hands, and wept.

Suddenly he heard footsteps outside the door. He raised his head and saw the door slowly swing open. To his astonishment he saw his daughter, dressed in her shroud, entering the room. She tottered across to where her father sat, threw herself upon his lap, and twined her arms around his neck. She nestled down in her stunned parent's arms, but a moment later fell slowly backward. He raised her up, but she sagged limply and lifelessly against him.

The first death had, in fact, been only a coma. The child was pronounced dead for the second time, and her body was buried that same day.

This macabre real-life story went across the ocean to London where it was published in the *Illustrated Police News*.

One of the most horrifying of all kinds of ghost stories concerns premature burial. The possibility of being interred while still alive but in a coma is a very real, and to some extent well-founded, fear. Today such an occurrence is extremely unlikely, although it does occasionally happen. In his book *The Romeo Error*, Lyall Watson cites a case that occurred in New York in 1964. A surgeon was about to perform a post-mortem examination when the supposed corpse leaped up and grabbed the surgeon by the throat. The surgeon died of shock.

Edgar Allan Poe was morbidly fascinated by the idea of premature burial, and this theme recurs in several of his stories. In one of the most macabre, "The Fall of the House of Usher," the master of the house, Roderick Usher, meets his death at the hands of a dead person. His sister, the Lady Madeline, has apparently died after a long wasting illness, and is installed in a vault in the lower regions of the decrepit mansion prior to final interment. Several nights later, in the midst of a violent storm, the deranged Roderick hears from below in the house the rending of her coffin, the creaking of the iron gate of the vault, and her footsteps on the stairs. Leaping to his feet he shrieks, " *'I tell you that she now stands without the door!'* "

At that moment the doors swing open slowly, and "there did stand the lofty and enshrouded figure of the Lady Madeline of Usher. There was blood upon her white robes, and the evidence of some bitter struggle upon every portion of her emaciated frame. For a moment she remained trembling and reeling to and fro upon the threshold, then, with a low moaning cry, fell heavily inward upon the person of her brother, and in her violent and now final death agonies, bore him to the floor a corpse, and a victim to the terrors he had anticipated."

In the best tradition of the horror story, the ghastly figure of Lady Madeline can be interpreted in more than one way: as a living woman who has crawled out of her own coffin; as the revengeful spirit of one who has suffocated in the tomb; or as the projection of Roderick's own guilt and fear.

The premature burial theme often appears in the persistent English legend of the moaning nun. The story has many variations, but a popular version concerns a nun who broke her vow of chastity and was punished by being buried alive within the convent walls. From this unconsecrated grave, her spirit ventures forth in an endless, futile quest for peace. In fact, many nuns and monks *were* buried secretly—after a natural death—inside the walls of manor houses to which they had fled for protection following the dissolution of the monasteries by Henry VIII. It may be that the legend of the immured nun grew out of stories of such actual cases of clandestine burial.

If so, it would not be the first time that the folk process had created a mythical ghost story around a kernel of fact. This process of distortion and embellishment goes on whenever any story is passed down by word of mouth. An example of the kind of distortion that takes place over the years is related in an article by the contemporary Scottish novelist Gordon M. Williams. While living in a hamlet in Devon, he heard of a local superstition that it is bad luck to die in mid-November. The manager of the local pub told him that "in the old days" dead

Above: a humorous treatment of a terrifying subject, the possibility of being buried alive. This 18th-century print depicts an exchange between a juror at an inquest and the coroner. The caption reads: "Juror: 'The man's alive, Sir, for he has opened one eye.' Coroner: 'Sir, the doctor declared him dead two hours since and he must remain dead, Sir, so I shall proceed with the inquest.'"
Left: a melodramatic treatment of premature burial: an illustration for Edgar Allan Poe's short story "The Fall of the House of Usher."

bodies had to be transported across the moor to the nearest graveyard, a distance of some 50 miles, for there was no consecrated graveyard nearby. Sometimes when the corpse was transported in winter, the carriers got caught in heavy snow on the wild moors and left the body packed in ice until the journey could be completed in spring. Thus, said the tavern keeper, the dead man was left alone, and without benefit of clergy, was the prey of any wandering demon that might pass his way. Inquiring when the last corpse had been transported, Williams was told by the pub keeper that it had happened "in my grandfather's time, or maybe my great grandfather's." Later, on checking the story in the British Museum, Williams found it to be basically true—with the significant difference that the last such corpse transportation had occurred in the year 1138.

In 1915 during World War I, the *Evening News* of London published a story by writer Arthur Machen describing an incident during the terrible retreat of the British army from Mons. Machen quoted an officer who claimed that, as he rode along with two other officers, he became aware of horsemen with longbows in the fields on either side. "So convinced were we that they were really cavalry, that at the next halt one of the officers took a party of men out to reconnoitre and found no one there." The phantom soldiers were assumed to be English bowmen from the field of Agincourt, where the English had won a great victory over the French in 1415. Interpreted this way, they were symbols of hope to the survivors of Mons.

Soon after the story was published, corroborative reports began to be circulated. In most of these stories, the phantom took the form of battalions of angels coming to the aid of the Allies. Machen confessed that his story was fiction; but by then the need to believe in the angels was too great to be denied. Soon almost every second survivor of Mons was telling his own version of the story; and there are still old men alive today who will swear that they saw the hosts of Heaven marching through gunsmoke toward the German lines.

An ironic postscript to the story was provided by Friedrich Herzenwirth, a former director of espionage for Germany, who claimed in his memoirs, published in 1930, that the angels were motion pictures. German pilots, he said, projected the images onto clouds in an attempt to make the English believe that God was on the side of the Kaiser.

The credulity of the human race, and its readiness to perpetuate colorful and dramatically satisfying ghost stories, has been something of a hindrance to serious psychical research. Hard-headed scientists have been reluctant to devote much attention to a field of research so permeated with old superstitions, literary clichés, and tourist attractions. The conviction persists among these skeptics that any haunting or apparition that can't be dismissed as myth can be ascribed to intoxication or mental instability on the part of the *percipient*—that is, the person who sees it.

Those researchers who have treated the subject seriously and scientifically have discovered plenty of cases that cannot be so easily dismissed. One of the earliest studies was the Census of Hallucinations, conducted by the Society for Psychical Research in 1890. The Census asked 17,000 people in Britain the following question: "Have you ever, when believing yourself to be completely awake, had a vivid impression of seeing or being touched by a living being or inanimate object, or of hearing a voice: which impression, so far as you could discover, was not due to any external physical cause?"

Of the 17,000 people that were polled, 1684, just under 10 per cent, answered "Yes." Similar studies were carried out in France, Germany, and the United States, and yielded an overall "Yes" response of 11.96 per cent from a total of some 27,000 replies. Those who answered "Yes" in the British survey were then asked to give as detailed an account as possible of their experience. They were carefully questioned and their stories evaluated by the SPR.

Above: this illustration from "Netley Abbey," one of the ghost stories in the *Ingoldsby Legends* written by R. H. Barham, shows a nun being immured in "a dungeon dark and drear!" presumably for having flirted with the gardener. Below: a picture from the *Illustrated Police News* of 1869 showing the discovery of a skeleton in the vaults of a medieval convent in southern Europe. Many stories of hauntings tie in with legends of people buried alive. Right: the parish church of Stoke Dry, Rutland, England. A compartment above the door is allegedly haunted by the ghost of a woman imprisoned there and starved to death for practicing witchcraft.

Above: the cover to a World War I song "Angel of Mons," based on a fictitious newspaper story that was widely believed to be fact.

Left: in the original story by Arthur Machen, the "angels" were English bowmen, supposedly spirits of those who had fallen in the Battle of Agincourt in 1415. As symbols of a great English victory, the mythical bowmen revived the morale of the defeated and exhausted soldiers at Mons, and soon eyewitness accounts of the ghostly phenomenon were appearing in the British press. They were taken as an omen of divine support for the Allies. Machen's revelation that his story was fiction make little impression on a populace who wanted desperately to believe in the angels.

Right: this drawing by Cruikshank shows a man who wakes in the middle of the night and gets scared by his own clothes, which he has draped over a chair and hung on the back of a door in such a way that they suggest two phantoms to his sleep-fogged brain. Countless cases of alleged hauntings have been proved to be optical illusions, just as many spectral footsteps turn out to be mice or the contraction of old timbers as a house cools at night.

The purpose of the Census was to test for telepathy—the hypothesis being that one person could somehow project an image of himself to another person. Many of the apparitions fell into this category; but others were of people known, or later discovered, to be dead.

Among the most interesting cases was that reported by Miss Morton (pseudonym), a medical student. For seven years between 1882 and 1889, her home was haunted by the figure of a tall woman wearing a dark dress. The ghost's routine was to walk down the stairs into the drawing room, stand for a moment beside the bow-window, leave the drawing room, and disappear through the door leading to the garden. Miss Morton saw and heard the figure on various occasions, and was able to describe it in some detail. It was, she said, "dressed in black of a soft woollen material, judging from the slight sound in moving. The face was hidden in a handkerchief. I saw the upper part of the left side of the forehead, and a little of the hair above. Her left hand was nearly hidden by her sleeve and a fold of her dress. As she held it down, a portion of a widow's cuff was visible. . . . There was no [widow's] cap on the head, but a general effect of blackness suggests a bonnet, with long veil or a hood." For the first two years, the apparition was so solid looking as to be mistaken for a living person. After 1884 it became less distinctive and appeared less often.

Several people beside Miss Morton saw the apparition, and their description of it tallied with her own. Her father, however, was unable to see it. Miss Morton provided the SPR with accounts of the figure's appearances, including this incident:

"The following evening, 12th August, while coming up the garden, I walked toward the orchard, when I saw the figure cross the orchard, go along the carriage drive in front of the house, and in at the open side door, across the hall and into the drawing room, I following. She crossed the drawing room and took up her usual position behind the couch in the bow window. My father came in soon after and I told him she was there. He could not see the figure, but went up to where I showed him she was. She then went swiftly around behind him, across the room, out of the door and along the hall, disappearing as usual near the garden door, we both following her. . . ."

Around 8 o'clock that same evening both Miss Morton and her sister saw the figure in the drawing room, where it remained by the window "for ten minutes or a quarter of an hour."

In an effort to understand the nature of the phenomenon, Miss Morton glued a piece of thread across the stairs; the figure passed through the thread without disturbing it. When she tried to touch the apparition, it always managed to be just beyond her reach. When she spoke to it, it would sometimes pause and look as though it were going to speak, but never did.

The description of the figure was found to resemble a Mrs. S. who had lived in the house until her death in 1878, although positive identification was impossible because the specter always partly covered her face with the handkerchief. The widow's weeds were one clue, Mr. S. having died two years before his wife, and the handkerchief held to the face might have been

Below: this man is not an extra in a ghost-story film, but an employee of the São Paulo, Brazil, traffic department which, in 1971, mounted a safety campaign to "spook" drivers into driving more carefully. Presumably the sight of a phantomlike figure weaving among the cars would remind drivers of their mortality.

Above: *The Ghost Story* depicts
a farmer entertaining his family
with a tale of the supernatural.
He has obviously just reached a
spine-chilling development, and
in a moment both he and his en-
thralled listeners will jump out
of their chairs in fright as the
jug crashes to the floor. In-
numerable supposed hauntings can
be traced to cats, whose stealthy
movements and glow-in-the-dark
eyes produce many ghostly effects.

Right: "It leapt towards him upon
the instant," an illustration of
the climatic moment of the ghost
story "Oh, Whistle, and I'll
Come to You, My Lad" by M. R.
James. The story tells of the experience of a skeptical professor
who, on a trip to the east coast
of England, finds an ancient
whistle, idly blows upon it, and
in so doing apparently conjures
up some evil spirit. Or has he
conjured up those superstitions
that lurk in his own subconscious
mind—perhaps an inherited racial
memory? The ambiguity in James'
narrative reflects the ambiguities
underlying the whole question of
ghosts as myth or reality.

another. The marriage had apparently been an unhappy one. Mr. S. had become a heavy drinker after the death of his first wife, and the second Mrs. S. not only failed in her attempt to reform him, but began to drink heavily herself. According to people who had known Mrs. S., the behavior and general appearance of the ghost seemed reminiscent of the unhappy, often intoxicated widow.

If you're inclined to regard Miss Morton's dark lady as a product of the Victorian death-obsessed culture, consider a simpler case that occurred in 1929. It was reported by Andrew MacKenzie in his book *Apparitions and Ghosts*. Mrs. Deane (pseudonym) was spending a weekend at the home of her daughter's nurse in Cleveland, Ohio. The nurse, called Mrs. Mills in the account, was a widow with a young son whom Mrs. Deane had met. Other than these facts, Mrs. Deane knew little of Mrs. Mills' family.

On the first evening of her visit, Mrs. Deane was undressing for bed when, in her own words, "I heard a sound at the bedroom door as if the knob were being turned, and on opening it saw a good-looking young girl, normally dressed, standing there. I said 'Hello, who are you?' to which she replied, 'I'm Lottie and this is my room,' but when I said 'Won't you come

The Woman Who Would Not Die

Ligeia, heroine of a story by that master of the macabre Edgar Allan Poe, was a woman with a fierce will to live. Nonetheless she died slowly of a wasting disease. In her last words she declared that it was only through weakness of will that humans gave in to death.

Her grief-stricken husband moved to England and tried to create a new life. He bought and renovated an old abbey, and remarried. In this loveless marriage he continued to be obsessed by memories of the dusky-haired and passionate Ligeia. After a few months his second wife fell ill and died.

As he kept watch by the body the hero suddenly detected a return of color to her cheeks. He tried to bring her back to life, but she quickly sank back into death. An hour later, a sigh issued from the supposed corpse, and once more he tried in vain to revive her. All through the night she fluctuated between life and death, and with each struggle she seemed to become more alive. Finally, toward morning, the shrouded figure rose and walked toward her husband. As she drew the shroud from her head, "there streamed forth ... huge masses of long and dishevelled hair ... blacker than the raven wings of midnight." It was Ligeia.

Right: a triumph of Victorian "spirit photography." The ghost of the mother, cut from another negative and suitably pared down to look ethereal, hovers over her sleeping child. Real apparitions cannot fly, any more than living people can, but they have sometimes been seen to walk up non-existent stairs that had existed when the person was alive.

Below: this German photo of the 1880s is one of the more obvious fakes of its kind. The skull is somewhat at variance with the Spiritualist belief that bodies on the other side are simply versions of our earthly bodies.

Above: more bogus photos of hauntings. The same country cottage and the same superimposed specter. Only the percipients are changed.

in?' she just smiled and entirely disappeared.

"Strangely, I did not feel at all nervous and slept quite soundly that night. In the morning I said to Mrs. Mills, 'Who's Lottie?' She replied, 'Lottie was my pet name for my daughter Charlotte who died a few years ago, but how did you know about her?'

"So I told her of the visit to my bedroom the night before. She showed me a photograph of Charlotte, who looked just as I had 'seen' her."

Mrs. Mills was very upset about the incident and reluctant to discuss her daughter. Some 40 years later, after Mrs. Deane reported the incident to him, Andrew MacKenzie tried to locate the record of the girl's death, but in spite of the cooperation of the Registrar in Cleveland, the attempt was unsuccessful. The year of death was not known, and could not be obtained because Mrs. Mills and her son could not be located.

Whether the figure outside the door had any connection with Charlotte Mills, it certainly was real enough, for a few moments, to Mrs. Deane. Perhaps it was only a draft in the hall that caused the noise of the doorknob being turned. Perhaps Mrs. Deane was in an agitated state at the time. Perhaps she only imagined the brief conversation with the girl. It would be hard to deny, however, that Mrs. Deane and all the thousands of other people whose ghost stories have been examined by psychical researchers, have had some contact with phenomena that can't as yet be explained by modern science.

Ghosts—whatever else they may be—are a fact of life.

Below: a ghost photograph that may be genuine. Mrs. Mabel Chinnery of Ipswich, England, took this picture of her husband in their car before they returned from the cemetery where they had been laying flowers on her mother's grave. When she received the prints of the film she found an image of her mother (arrowed) in the back seat. The photographic expert of the *Sunday Pictorial*, the paper that published the picture in 1959, declared that it was genuine, and a psychical researcher, Tom Hardiman Scott, said: "There appears to be no natural explanation for this remarkable photograph."

2

Alarms and Predictions

One day around the middle of the last century, a little girl of about 10 was walking along a country lane in England not far from her home. Evidently rather advanced for her age, she was reading a book on geometry. Suddenly the scene in front of her faded away, and she saw in its place the bedroom in her house known as the White Room. Her mother was lying on the floor, apparently dead. The vision was complete and vivid, and it remained before her eyes for several minutes. Then gradually it faded away. So convincing was the scene that the child went immediately to the family doctor and persuaded him to accompany her home. When

This illustration for "Barbara of the Shining Garments," a Christmas ghost story, shows a crisis apparition of a young woman at the point of death. The fact that so many apparitions are of people who, at the moment they are seen, are undergoing some physical or mental crisis has led psychical researchers to draw the conclusion that the apparition is a kind of message sent telepathically from the person undergoing the crisis to the person who sees the figure.

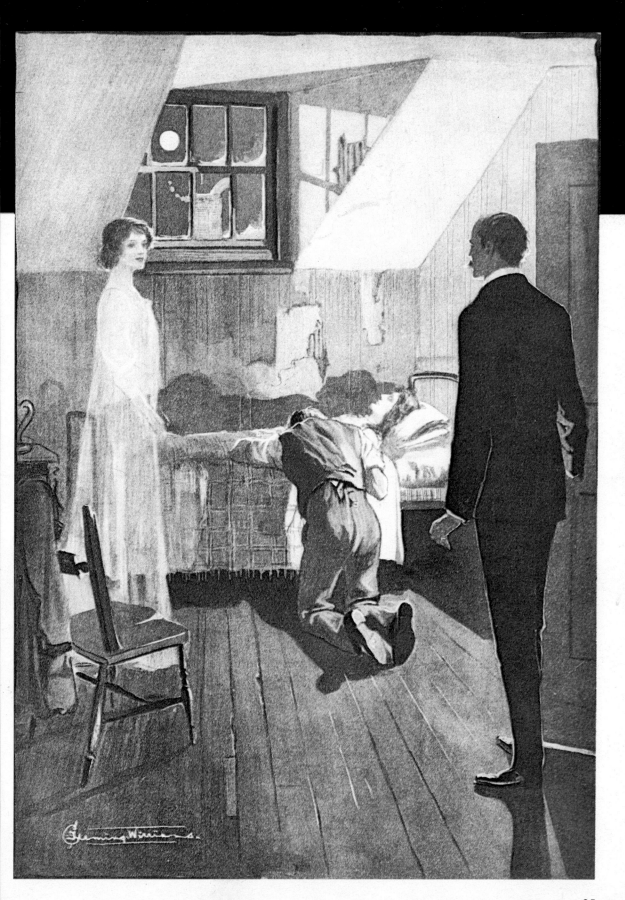

"The sender is probably unconscious of sending the message"

they arrived at the house, they and the girl's father went straight to the White Room. There they found the child's mother lying on the floor. She had suffered a heart attack, and the arrival of the doctor at that moment saved her life. This case, reported in *Phantasms of the Living* by Gurney, Myers, and Podmore, is significant not only because the image was confirmed by reality—even down to a detail such as a lace-edged handkerchief lying beside the woman, but also because the mother had apparently been perfectly well at the time the child left the house. The girl herself was not at all anxious about her mother until she saw the vision, and the father, corroborating the story, stated that he had been surprised to find the doctor at the door and had asked, "Who is ill?" The facts suggest that the vision had somehow been transmitted to the child by her mother at the moment of the crisis.

A vision of a person who, at the time, is undergoing some traumatic experience such as severe illness, injury, or death, is known as a "crisis apparition." Put simply, the theory behind the phenomenon is that the person undergoing the crisis telepathically sends a picture of himself to someone with whom he has a close relationship, and that if that person is sufficiently sensitive he will pick up the picture. The sender, or "agent," is probably unconscious of sending the message, though in the case of a death crisis we have no way of discovering whether or not this is true. Some psychical researchers prefer to include apparitions seen several hours after death in the category of "delayed" crisis apparitions, and to suggest that the agent transmitted the

Below: this old German engraving shows the apparition of a drowned traveler appearing to his wife. The housekeeper, at left, is just rushing in with news of the tragedy. An unusual feature of this case is that the man is naked; almost all apparitions are clothed.

picture while still alive — even if at the point of death.

A typical case of a delayed crisis apparition, discussed by G. N. M. Tyrrell in his book *Apparitions*, was experienced by a Mrs. Paquet whose brother worked on a tugboat in Chicago's harbor. One day Mrs. Paquet awoke feeling unaccountably depressed, and could not shake the mood off. Having gone into the pantry for some tea, she saw her brother Edmund standing a few feet away from her as she turned around. "The apparition stood with back toward me, or, rather, partially so, and was in the act of falling forward—away from me—seemingly impelled by two loops or a loop of rope drawing against his legs. The vision lasted but a moment, disappearing over a low railing or bulwark, but was very distinct. I dropped the tea, clasped my hands to my face, and exclaimed, 'My God! Ed is drowned.'" Soon after this experience, she received the news that her brother had fallen overboard and drowned, exactly as she saw it happen, but about six hours before her vision.

If a person can involuntarily project his image at a moment of crisis, it would seem possible that some people might be able to do so voluntarily through a great effort of will and concentration. Various people have tried this, occasionally with success. Around the turn of the century a Mr. Kirk made some attempts at transmitting his own image to a friend referred to as Miss G. These experiments were reported in the *Proceedings* of the SPR.

Over a period of 10 days between the hours of 11 p.m. and 1 a.m. every night, Mr. Kirk concentrated on making himself visible to Miss G.—without, of course, letting her know of his experiment. Several times during this period he saw Miss G., and although she complained of being restless and having trouble sleeping, she reported no apparitions. It was not until some days after Mr. Kirk stopped the experiment that she revealed she had seen him in her room—not at night but during one afternoon.

It had been on June 11 around 3:30 or 4:00 p.m. Mr. Kirk had been at his office doing some auditing work, and had begun to feel rather tired. He leaned back and stretched, and on an impulse decided to try his telepathy experiment. Not knowing where Miss G. might be at the moment, he chose her bedroom. What happened next was reported to the SPR by Miss G.

"In the afternoon (being tired by a morning walk) while sitting in an easy chair near the window of my own room, I fell asleep," she said. "At any time I happen to sleep during the day . . . I invariably awake with tired uncomfortable sensations, which take some little time to pass off; but that afternoon, on the contrary, I was suddenly quite wide awake, seeing Mr. Kirk standing near my chair, dressed in a dark-brown coat, which I had frequently seen him wear. [Mr. Kirk reported that he was wearing that coat at the time, although he seldom wore it in the office.] His back was toward the window, his right hand toward me; he passed across the room toward the door . . . but when he got about four feet from the door, which was closed, he disappeared . . . I then thought, knowing he must be at the office at the time I saw him . . . that in this instance, at least, it must be purely imaginary, and feeling so sure it was only fancy, resolved not to mention it, and did not do so until this week when, almost involuntarily, I told him about it.

Below: an apparition called the "enfant brillant" appearing to Lord Castlereagh while he was visiting a friend in Northern Ireland. The future Foreign Minister awoke in the middle of the night and saw a lovely shining figure of a child by his bed. He approached the child, who gradually disappeared. Castlereagh is also said to have seen the child once in the House of Commons and again on the day he committed suicide.

Much more difficult to account for is the case of a Mrs. Crone of west London who, one day in 1951, was working in her kitchen when she saw the image of a friend who lived in southeast London. She saw only the head and shoulders of this woman, whom we'll call Miss A., but was struck by the extremely anxious look on her face. Somehow the apparition made Mrs. Crone suspect that her own little boy might be in trouble, and she hurried to the dining room where she had left him in his baby carriage.

The baby, who was strong for his 18 months, had managed to rock the carriage over to a sideboard, had taken several knives including some carving knives from a drawer, and had put them in the carriage. Mrs. Crone quickly rescued him.

Reporting the incident to psychical researcher Andrew MacKenzie, who included it in *Apparitions and Ghosts*, Mrs. Crone expressed her surprise that the warning should come from Miss A., who was not a close friend. In fact, Mrs. Crone never told Miss A. of the event. At the time she saw the apparition, Mrs. Crone was, in her own words, "not thinking of anything in particular," but "when you have a young child he is never far from your mind." She had on other occasions seen images of people, always just of the head and shoulders. In view of her psychic tendency, it would not have been too surprising had she seen an image of her son reaching for the knives. Why, then, did she see a vision of Miss A instead?

Another kind of apparition is a curious one called the "false-arrival" hallucination. In such a case the percipient sees, or usually just hears, another person arrive—the opening of the gate, footsteps on the path, the opening of the front door—perhaps half an hour or an hour before the person actually arrives. The true arrival is an exact repetition of the false one—except that the person is really there. Apparently this phenomenon is fairly common in Scandinavian countries. A professor of physics at the University of Oslo who has investigated such occurrences has discovered that the false arrival usually is heard at the time the person is deciding to set out on his journey. He speculates that this is a form of communication that has evolved especially among people who live in isolated rural areas.

A sparsely populated part of England, the Norfolk Fen district, was the scene of a visible case of false-arrival, included in *Phantasms of the Living*. The story concerned two brothers who had married two sisters, and who lived with their respective families about a mile and a quarter apart. One day, a friend who was visiting one of the brothers glanced out the window and said, "Here is your brother coming." The friend's report continues:

"My host advanced to the window and said, 'Oh, yes. Here he is; and see, Robert has got Dobbin out at last.' Dobbin was a horse, which, on account of some accident, had not been used for some weeks. The lady also looked out of the window, and said to me, 'And I am so glad, too, that my sister is with him. They will be delighted to find you here.' I recognized distinctly the vehicle in

A Glimpse of the Future

At the age of 22 the German poet Johann Wolfgang von Goethe had completed his studies in Strasbourg and was about to return home. While in Strasbourg he had fallen in love with the daughter of a pastor in a nearby village. He loved her but didn't want to be tied.

He paid one last visit to his Fredericka before leaving the town. "When I reached her my hand from my horse, the tears stood in her eyes and I felt sad at heart," he wrote in his autobiography. Then, as he rode away, he had a strange vision. "I saw, not with the eyes of the body, but with those of the mind, my own figure coming toward me on horseback, and on the same road, attired in a suit which I had never worn—pike gray with gold lace. As soon as I shook myself out of this dream the figure had entirely disappeared . . . eight years afterward, I found myself on the very road, to pay one more visit to Fredericka, in the suit of which I had dreamed."

Although the phenomenon of seeing one's doppelgänger is traditionally regarded as a death omen, Goethe did not interpret his experience in that way. "However it may be with matters of this kind generally, this strange illusion in some measure calmed me at the moment of parting."

Left: two lovers of the Middle Ages meet their doppelgängers, or ghostly doubles, in this romantic painting by Rossetti. The sight of one's doppelgänger was, according to legend, an omen of death. Rossetti's flesh-and-blood lovers react to the sight with terror.

which they rode . . . also the lady and gentleman."

The visitors turned the corner, and disappeared along the side of the house. Inside the others waited for a knock on the door, but none came. The host expressed astonishment that his brother and sister-in-law had passed by the house without stopping in, "a thing they never did in their lives before." A few minutes later the niece, a young woman of 25, burst into the house, very upset. "Oh, aunt, I have had such a fright," she said. "Father and Mother have passed me on the road without speaking. I looked up at them as they passed by, but they looked straight on and never stopped nor said a word. A quarter of an hour before, when I started to walk here, they were sitting by the fire; and now what can be the matter? They never turned or spoke, and yet I am certain that they must have seen me."

About 10 minutes later, the carriage and its occupants were seen again, heading in the same direction. This time they actually arrived in the flesh. At the time the phantom was seen, the couple were just beginning their journey.

An Englishwoman, Miss J.B., recounts a case of a ghost seen years in advance of its arrival.

"When I was a small child in Yorkshire, just after the First World War, I lived with my parents in a large old farmhouse in the Dales. . . . The kitchen was my favorite place, and on winter days I spent most of my time at the kitchen table drawing and painting while the daily help bustled around preparing meals. I must have been about six when I saw my 'ghost.' She was thin and pale, with long dark hair tied in a bun at the nape of her neck, and she stood by the kitchen range sobbing and muttering in a language which I could not understand.

"Her dress was gray and worn, and her shoes were in need of mending, but she had an air of gentility about her. When I mentioned the 'lady in gray' both my mother and the 'help' seemed surprised, and I think they must have thought that I was day-dreaming."

Miss J.B. saw the figure again about a year later, and subsequently came across her, always weeping, about nine or 10 times during the next few years. "For some reason I never spoke to her; I got the impression that she needed sympathy, but that I would be unable to help her. By this time I was certain that she was a ghost, but I felt no fear of her. I used to slip out of the kitchen and leave her to her misery."

Shortly after her 14th birthday, Miss J.B. went to live with an uncle in Ireland, and remained there throughout World War II. She returned to Yorkshire in 1945.

"I was driven to the old house from Leeds by my mother who explained that, as the place was too big for her since my father's death, she had a family of Polish refugees staying—a mother and two young daughters. The father, she said, had vanished during the German occupation, and the mother was still grief-stricken over his loss. When we entered the kitchen there—to my astonishment—was the 'lady in gray' of my youth, standing by the kitchen range, weeping.

"Two little girls were standing near her, hanging onto her skirts, but apart from this she was exactly as I remembered her. She dried her eyes as we came into the room, and forced a smile."

Above: an illustration from S. Baring-Gould's short story "Mustapha," which contains a ghostly prediction of death. The young Englishman has tricked Mustapha, an Egyptian, into breaking a vow never to drink anymore. He had made the vow to fulfill his obligations as a Moslem, and so win the girl he loved. After breaking it, he feels honor-bound to cut his own throat, but his ghost haunts the guilty young Englishman, who is eventually found dead—his throat cut—in front of the mosque.

Above: *Saul and the Witch of Endor*, a depiction of the scene in I Samuel in which King Saul, whose nation is threatened by the Philistines, asks the witch to conjure up the spirit of his father Samuel in order to gain his counsel. The ghost of Samuel rebukes Saul for not obeying the voice of the Lord, and predicts that he will be vanquished by the Philistines—a prediction that comes true.

Below: the Roman leader Brutus is visited in his tent by a specter who is his own evil spirit. According to myth, it visited him again the night before he was defeated and killed at Philippi.

When she got to know the woman better, Miss J.B. tried to explain to her about the vision, but as her guest spoke only a little English, she was never able to understand. "What did happen, though, was that because I seemed to know her as an old acquaintance, I think I was better able to comfort her and give her reassurance in her new country."

Miss J.B. thinks that the vision she had as a child was not transmitted by the Polish woman herself, whose grief, after all, was not caused until years after the apparitions occurred, "but from some benign intelligence—Heaven or God if you like—that, with the knowledge of what was to come, wanted to build up sympathy in me in advance."

If the vision was not projected by any intelligence, and if it was not a product of the child's own mind that just happened to resemble the Polish woman, we are left with the idea that there is another kind of time coexisting with the time we know, and that somehow a moment in the future overlapped *visibly* with a moment in the present as experienced by the young girl. The theory of different systems of time is an extremely complex and difficult subject, beyond the scope of this book. But every now and then one encounters a ghost story—like that of the Polish woman—which strongly suggests that the future can be seen.

Wing Commander George Potter looked into the future one evening during World War II, and did not like what he saw. At the time he was a squadron leader stationed at a base called R.A.F. Shallufa in Egypt. From this base, light bombers flew out over the Mediterranean to plant torpedoes and mines in the paths of the German General Rommel's supply ships. Because the squadron operated at night, they usually flew during the "bomber's moon" period when the bright reflection of the full moon on the sea helped them to navigate.

The atmosphere on the base between bombing periods was one of nervous gaiety. Pilots, navigators, gunners, and bombardiers spent their leisure evenings drinking and smoking.

On one such evening, just before the bomber's moon came again, Potter entered the mess with Flying Officer Reg Lamb for a nightcap. He glanced idly around the room, noting who was there. Among those present was a wing commander whom Potter, in telling the story, calls Roy. He was surrounded by friends.

Potter and Lamb finished their drinks, and Potter bought another round. As he did so, he heard a burst of laughter from the group around Roy, and it made him glance their way.

"Then," he says, "I saw it. I turned and saw the head and shoulders of the wing commander moving ever so slowly in a bottomless depths of blue-blackness. His lips were drawn back from his teeth in a dreadful grin; he had eye-sockets but no eyes; the remaining flesh of his face was dully blotched in greenish, purplish shadows, with shreds peeling off near his left ear.

"I gazed. It seemed that my heart had swollen and stopped. I experienced all the storybook sensations of utter horror. The hair on my temples and the back of my neck felt like wire, icy sweat trickled down my spine, and I trembled slightly all over. I was vaguely aware of faces nearby, but the horrible death mask dominated the lot.

Afterward Potter had no recollection of how long the experience lasted, but he gradually became aware of Flying Officer Lamb tugging at his sleeve. "What the hell's the matter?" Lamb asked. "You've gone as white as a sheet . . . as if you've seen a ghost!"

"I *have* seen a ghost," said Potter, pointing a trembling finger. "Roy. Roy has the mark of death on him."

Reg Lamb looked over to where Roy and the others were gathered. He saw nothing unusual; but by his side the normally unshakable Potter was still ashen-faced and unsteady. Both of them knew that Roy would be flying on the following night, and Potter did not know what, if anything, to do.

"I was in a quandary," he says, "but I think I made the right decision. I decided against going to the group captain with my story in the hope that Roy would be withdrawn from the mission, and I am certain that Roy himself would have refused to be kept from his crew. I am convinced that the decision not to interfere was . . . part of a preordained sequence of events."

The following night was a tense one for Potter. Toward morning the telephone shrilled, and he snatched the receiver from its cradle. The message: Roy and his crew had been shot down, but their plane had been seen to ditch safely, and a companion air-

Left: the ghost of the first Duke of Buckingham is shown in this engraving appearing to a servant of his son, the second Duke. The armor-clad figure told the servant to warn his son—a notorious libertine who had killed a man in a duel—to mend his ways, or face his own death. On three occasions the ghost visited the servant, the last time carrying a dagger. The message was conveyed to the son—who made no attempt to reform and was assassinated six months later.

craft had circled above while they clambered into a life raft.

"I felt an enormous sense of relief and elation," says Potter. "The air-sea rescue boys would soon have them out of it. But my elation was short-lived. They searched and searched, but no one ever saw Roy and his crew again. And then I knew what I had seen; the blue-black nothingness was the Mediterranean Sea at night, and he was floating somewhere in it, dead, with just his head and shoulders held up by his Mae West."

The vivid, accurate details of the terrible vision suggest that Potter had, for a moment, been able to look into the future. Another kind of supernatural prediction of death is that in which an apparition of someone known to be dead warns the percipient of his own approaching death. Such ghostly warnings are com-

Above: the ghost of the Earl of Strafford, who is supposed to have appeared to several people including King Charles I. Strafford's ghost warned the king not to take on Cromwell's forces at Naseby the next day. The king disregarded the warning and was defeated. Left: Dunstaffnage Castle near Oban, Scotland. Its owner, Mr. Campbell, spends one night here every year—even though the castle is not only uncomfortable but also haunted. One of its 15 ghosts, the Gray Man, is said to presage death.

Above: Martin Luther, the German Protestant reformer whose ghost is supposed to have appeared to an Englishman who had agreed to translate Luther's discourses into English. Luther himself was said to have seen apparitions, but was inclined to attribute such things to the cunning of evil spirits.

mon enough in fiction, but they occasionally occur in real life as well. An apparition of this kind—if later fulfilled—suggests not only that it is possible to see into the future but also that the apparition and warning have been projected by a surviving personality, who knows in advance what will happen.

The ghost seen by Mrs. Gertrude Ashimi appeared in a dream, which makes it less startling than a waking hallucination.

Born in a small township in Nigeria of a prosperous family, Mrs. Ashimi was taken to Europe as a child, and educated by Roman Catholic nuns. Later she studied law in London, and in 1968, after qualifying as a lawyer, she returned to Nigeria for a visit with her widowed mother and brothers.

One morning, Mrs. Ashimi told her family that she had had a vivid dream. She had seen an old, smiling woman who, she was certain, was her maternal grandmother—although she had never seen her. In her right hand the old woman held a gold crucifix with a pearl in its center, attached to a fine gold chain. "My grandmother beckoned for me to follow, and walked out into the garden where she pointed to a certain tree. She tapped with her foot on the ground near the base of the tree and said, 'It is here, for you.' Then she vanished."

At her description of the old woman, Mrs. Ashimi's mother became excited. It was certainly her own mother, she said. What was more, the chain and crucifix sounded exactly like the one that the old woman had worn, and that had vanished shortly before her death. The whole family went into the garden and gathered around the tree to which the woman in the dream had pointed, while Gertrude Ashimi began to dig in the hard-baked earth. A few inches down she found the cross and chain.

Mrs. Ashimi returned to London with her husband, also a lawyer, and they set up a legal practice. In 1972, while awaiting the birth of her baby in a London hospital, she told a friend the story of the crucifix which she wore around her neck. She also told the friend that she had "an uneasy feeling" about the baby, for once again her grandmother had appeared to her in a dream and this time the old woman was not smiling but sad-faced. Mrs. Ashimi was 27 and in robust health, and she gave birth to a fine little boy. A few days after the birth, however, she died suddenly.

Not all spectral predictions involve death. John Aubrey, a 17th-century English gentleman who collected anecdotes about prominent people of his day, recounts a curious story of a spirit who may or may not have been the ghost of Martin Luther.

Back in the 16th century Luther's discourses had been banned by the Pope after he excommunicated the reformer as a heretic. The order was that all copies should be burned, and the penalty for disobedience was death. (The ban, of course, did not apply in those German states that adopted the Lutheran faith.) During the turmoil of the religious wars in Germany in the early 17th century, a Lutheran named Caspar von Sparr discovered a copy of the discourses, and decided that the best way to preserve them was to smuggle them to England where they could be translated into English and republished. He entrusted the task of doing this to an English diplomat named Captain Bell, and Bell accordingly took the book with him to London.

Bell was a busy man, however, and months went by while the

book lay unopened and gathering dust in his library. Then one night he awoke with a start to see a gaunt figure standing by his bed; its bones stood out from the transparent flesh, and a long white beard hung down to its waist. To Bell's horror the phantom suddenly shot out a hand and nipped his ear in an amazingly firm grasp between finger and thumb.

"Sirrah!" it roared, "will you not take time to translate that book which is sent you out of Germany? I will provide you both a place and a time to do it!" With that it vanished, leaving Bell wiping the cold sweat from his forehead and nursing a sore ear. The ghost was as good as its word—or perhaps it simply had a gift for prediction. A few days later, after an unforseen disagreement with the Lord Chancellor, Bell was thrown into prison and left there without trial for 10 years. With nothing else to do, he settled down to translating Luther's discourses.

Was the apparition the spirit of Martin Luther? It certainly didn't look like him, and its command of English was somewhat remarkable for a German of that day. Perhaps it was one of Luther's more ardent followers, or simply a projection of Bell's conscience. One wishes the SPR had been there to investigate.

Above: the lecherous Lord Lyttleton is visited by the ghost of Mrs. Amphlett, whose two daughters Lyttleton had seduced. "Prepare to die, my Lord, you will quickly be called," she warned, adding that within three days he would be "in the state of the departed." Three nights later, his friend Mr. Andrews awoke to find a familiar but spectral face poking through the bed curtains. "Ah, Andrews," murmured Lyttleton's ghost, "it's all over." Andrews later learned that at the moment the head appeared in his room, Lyttleton had just collapsed, dead, in the arms of a servant. The story became a favorite of ghost story anthologies, and the theme of the ghost as moral avenger was very popular with 19th-century illustrators.

3

Haunts

Lieutenant John Scollay was normally an even-tempered man, but at the moment he was losing patience with his sergeant-major. Here, in a little wood outside Dunkirk, Scollay was trying to hold his company together in the face of sporadic but deadly German sniper fire. Too many of the green-kilted Scottish Highlanders had crumpled into the undergrowth that day in June 1940, and now, as night fell, the sergeant-major's absurd notion cracked Scollay's calm.

"What the bloody hell do you mean, *haunted*?" he snapped. "This wood is haunted by Huns, laddie, that's all you need to know and think about at the moment."

Above: the inn sign of the Cannard's Grave Inn, Somerset, England. Cannard, an innkeeper, became rich by dealing with highwaymen and smugglers. When he tried forgery, he was found out. Rather than submit to justice, he hanged himself. He was buried at the crossroads where his gang of footpads had ambushed travelers, and where the inn stands today. His ghost now haunts the spot.

Right: a painting of a phantom battle seen by the inhabitants of Verviers, Belgium in June, 1815, within a month of the actual Battle of Waterloo.

"Some research ...uncovered a significant fact"

The sergeant-major was persistent. "The wood is haunted, sir," he whispered. "I know it and the lads know it. For the love of God, sir, we're no' scared of Germans. If we have to we'll advance, or we'll force a way through the Jerries on our flank—but we canna stay here another night!"

Ridiculous as the idea sounded, Scollay couldn't entirely dismiss it. For the past 48 hours his company had been holed up in this straggling thicket. They were surrounded by fields in which German soldiers were entrenched awaiting the arrival of tanks, which would mean the end for the little band of Scots. During those two days, the Highlanders had fought with their usual cheerful savagery, raking the enemy with Bren gun fire and cracking off rifle shots at any moving shadow. Now they seemed to be losing their morale—an unheard of occurrence among the 51st Highlanders. Because of *ghosts*?

"It's just a presence, sir," explained the sergeant-major, "but we've all felt it. It's a kind of force pushing us away. And it's something that none of us can fight sir—something uncanny."

Eventually the 51st dropped back, joining the other British troops in the disastrous retreat from Dunkirk. Once clear of the "haunted wood" Scollay's men regained their determination and high spirits, but against the Panzer tanks and Stuka dive-bombers they could do nothing. Most of them were either slain or taken prisoner on the dunes of Dunkirk.

Scollay himself spent the duration of the war in a German P.O.W. camp, where he occasionally pondered the words of the sergeant-major on that night in June. When the war ended, he went back to the "haunted wood." Some research in a Dunkirk library uncovered a significant fact: in the summer of 1415, a few months before the Battle of Agincourt, English soldiers had fought the French in that same thicket.

Had the spirits of the slain English and French soldiers whose bodies had lain in the underbrush somehow come back

Below: *The Heroes of Marathon*, a painting depicting the battle between Greeks and Persians in 490 B.C. According to legend, the battle was reenacted by ghostly combatants every night for several years after the Greek victory there.

to haunt their successors, more than 500 years later? Or was the area permeated with an aura of death, which the Scots began to sense after two days of exposure to it? There was no local tradition of haunting on that spot, but perhaps the psychic force had lain dormant for five centuries to manifest only under the stimulus of fresh violence.

Scollay is not sure what that force was, but he is convinced of its existence. "There could never be any question of the courage of those men in battle," he says. "Their valor is a matter of record. But something more than gunfire frightened the hell out of them that day."

If that little wood in northern France is haunted, it is only one of the battlefields with supernatural reputations. According to legend, the battlefield of Marathon was such a place. For several years following the Greeks' victory over the Persians there in 492 B.C., the battle was mysteriously repeated every night. Anyone visiting the field after sunset heard the clash of steel upon steel and the screams of the wounded and dying, and smelled the odor of blood. Those who were unfortunate enough actually to see the ghostly warriors reportedly died within the year.

Spectral battles are a dramatic example of the kind of apparition we call a haunting. When most people think of ghosts they think of the kind that appear over and over in the same place. The "single-appearance" apparition, such as a crisis apparition, is less familiar. A ghost that appears to one person—or even a group of people—at one time only is a private kind of ghost. But a ghost that is associated with a particular place and has been seen there more than once is a ghost that might be seen by anyone. Moreover, the haunting ghost usually has a dramatic story behind it—some reason why the person's spirit, or image, seems to be fixed there. The supposed reason for the haunt is usually found to be either great unhappiness experienced by

Above: the surrender of the 51st Highland Division to Field Marshal Rommel (left) at Saint Valery-en-Caux, France, shortly after the Allied defeat at Dunkirk in June 1940. A peculiar incident in the battle was experienced by a small group of the Highlanders. They became convinced that the thicket in which they were fending off the surrounding Germans was haunted.

Left: the English cavalry in a painting of *The Morning of the Battle of Agincourt*. The supposedly haunted thicket where some Highlanders fought in 1940 had been the scene of an English-French skirmish shortly before Agincourt. Could it have been ghosts of that encounter that the Scots perceived 500 years later?

41

Left: an engraving of the English Civil War battle at Edgehill in 1642. For several months after the battle people reported seeing a phantom reenactment of it. The ghostly forces included Prince Rupert, commander of the Royalist troops (left), who was still alive when the apparition was seen.

the person in that place, or great emotional attachment to the place, or some form of violence.

Following this line of thought, we can assume that if *any* place is haunted, a battlefield surely would be. The pain and terror once concentrated there, the pride in victory and shame in defeat, not to mention the prodigious energy expended by the men would somehow be impressed on the spot, capable of being sensed or even seen and heard by people with sufficient psychic awareness. If this theory is correct, one would expect all battlefields to be haunted, but relatively few of them have this reputation.

Of such battlefield hauntings, one of the most famous took place in England at Edgehill, Warwickshire. There, on October 23, 1643, Royalist troops commanded by the King's nephew, Prince Rupert, and Parliamentarian troops under Oliver Cromwell fought the first battle of the English Civil War. After the battle, which was indecisive, the bodies of some 5000 men lay on the frozen ground of Edgehill.

A month after the battle some local shepherds saw a strange sight—the soldiers of King and Parliament locked once more in struggle, drums beating, harnesses creaking, cannons belching shot and smoke. This time, however, there were no bodies left on the ground. When the phantom armies were seen again, on Christmas Eve, news of the phenomenon was sent to Charles I. The King ordered several officers, some of whom had fought at Edgehill, to go and investigate.

On their return the officers brought detailed confirmation of the news. Not only had they interviewed the shepherds and recorded their accounts in detail, but they had also on two occasions seen the battle themselves. They recognized some of the men known to have died at Edgehill. They also recognized the figure of Prince Rupert, who was very much alive. Whether or not anyone took notice of it at the time, this particular observation was a strong piece of evidence for the theory that

ghosts are not the spirits of the departed, but rather a kind of recording of a scene that is left to be replayed under certain circumstances.

King Charles interpreted the ghostly battle as an omen that the rebellion against him would soon be put down—an interpretation that was proved wrong six years later when Cromwell's party assumed power and had the King beheaded.

The American Civil War was perhaps the greatest tragedy in the history of the United States, and we might expect its battlefields to echo with this terrible conflict that swallowed up the lives of nearly half a million men. Yet the Civil War battlefields remain, for the most part, silent. Occasionally a story surfaces about phantom troops at Gettysburg, but the only Civil War battlefield widely reputed to be haunted is Shiloh. This spot in Tennessee was where General Johnston's Confederates surprised the encamped army of General Grant on April 6, 1862. After two days' fighting, in which more than 24,000 men were killed, the Union Army defeated the Confederates. The river is said to have run deep pink with blood for days afterward. As soon as the terrible debris of battle had been cleared away,

Left: a painting of the American Civil War Battle at Shiloh. More than 24,000 soldiers were killed in this battle, a hard-won Union victory and one of the few Civil War battles reputed to have left ghosts of soldiers at the scene.

Below: a 1920 illustration of a Ku Klux Klan gathering. Members of the original Klan often pretended to be the ghosts of Shiloh.

Right: a portrait believed to be of Katherine Howard, fourth wife of Henry VIII. She was beheaded. Far right: the Haunted Gallery at Hampton Court Palace, which echoes with the shrieks of Katherine Howard's ghost (superimposed on the photo). She rushes along it and passes through the door at the end leading into the chapel. The haunting recalls a scene of Katherine's last days when she fled from the room where she was confined to beg for Henry's mercy.

Left: Windsor Castle is said to have several royal ghosts, including Charles I, George III, and Elizabeth I. She was first seen there a few days after her death at Richmond Palace, walking in the library. Some people have reported seeing the ghost of Queen Bess on the castle walls.

Below: a portrait of an unknown lady believed to be Ann Boleyn, by Holbein. Anne, Henry VIII's second wife, was imprisoned in the Tower of London and beheaded on the accusation of infidelity. Her ghost haunts the Tower as well as other places she lived.

rumors began to circulate of phantom armies appearing on the field every now and then—rumors that persist even today.

Whether real or imaginary, the ghosts of Shiloh indirectly aided the founding and early success of the Ku Klux Klan. The legend of the ghosts spread into other Southern states, being elaborated as it was retold. The spirits of Confederate soldiers, according to the story, were riding back to their homelands, where they would terrorize anyone who tried to change the traditional way of life.

The defeat of the South in 1865 put an end to that way of life—the most radical change being the freeing of hundreds of thousands of slaves. The white southerners feared the anger of this unleashed force, but soon some of them accidentally hit upon a way of frightening the blacks into passivity. A few ex-Confederate officers, who had formed a little club, rode drunkenly one night through the streets of Pulaski, Tennessee, draped in sheets. When they heard that many of the blacks had taken them for the legendary Shiloh dead, the group, who then called themselves the Kuklos Klan (*Kuklos* being the Greek for "circle"), realized the possibilities of their disguise. Throughout the Reconstruction period, the raids of the white-sheeted and hooded "ghosts" kept the black population effectively intimidated.

A real ghost can be seen anywhere—in broad daylight, in the most commonplace surroundings. Many ordinary houses, some of them quite new, are haunted. But the ghost stories that achieve wide fame are the ones connected with great and often gloomy houses, ruined abbeys, and castles. If the ghost is a royal personage, so much the better. There is a rather flimsy legend, for example, that the ghost of Queen Elizabeth I has appeared in the Queen's Library in Windsor Castle. The ghost of Katherine Howard, the fifth wife of Henry VIII, is said to run screaming through the rooms of Hampton Court Palace.

The Tower of London is saturated with pain and suffering endured by the victims of royal displeasure in the bad old days, and it has its share of ghost stories, though few of these are well authenticated. One story concerns the chapel of St. Peter-ad-Vincula, one of two chapels within the Tower, which is supposed to be the burial place of Henry's second wife, Anne Boleyn. Like her successor Katherine Howard, she was charged with infidelity, which was treason, and beheaded. One night a sentry, spotting a light in the chapel, climbed up to investigate along with another officer. Inside the chapel they saw a procession of people in Tudor dress walking up and down the aisles, led by a figure resembling Anne Boleyn. After a while, the figures and the light vanished.

We may hear these picturesque royal ghost stories with a skeptical smile. They are so transparently the products of wishful thinking. Yet they have a certain logic. If a haunting is caused in some way by a concentration of intense emotion in a particular spot, then whose figures would be likelier to appear than those of the people who were caught up in the ruthless intrigues and conflicts of their time? If one believes in ghosts at all, one can easily believe that the ghost of the unhappy Anne Boleyn, awaiting execution for a crime of which she is generally

Right: Littlecote, a manor house in Wiltshire, is haunted by several ghosts including the figure of a midwife clutching a baby who, according to a ghastly story, was thrown into the fire by his own father, "Wild Will Darrell," in 1575. Darrell's own ghost reputedly haunts the spot where he was thrown from his horse and killed.

Below: the ruins of old Scotney Castle in Kent. Another branch of the Darrell family (here spelled Darell) owned Scotney for more than 250 years. At the funeral of Arthur Darell in 1720, the coffin was being lowered into the grave when a stranger in a black coat, unknown to the mourners, said, "That is me they think they are burying." The man was never seen again, but a century or more later, the sexton opened an old coffin and found it filled with heavy stones. Arthur Darell's ghost does not haunt Scotney, but villagers say that every now and then the ghost of a drowned excise collector crawls out of the moat.

thought to have been innocent, and having indirectly caused the torture and death of several of her friends, might well become imprinted on the atmosphere of the Tower.

Britain is often said to be the most haunted country in the world. Actually, it is probably no more or less haunted than any other country, but as a people who cherish their traditions, the British do more than other nations to keep their ghosts alive so to speak. There is scarcely a country house from one tip of the island to the other without its resident phantom.

The ghosts of Littlecote, a manor in Wiltshire, recall a tragic and gory incident of Elizabethan days. In the 16th century the mansion belonged to "Wicked" Will Darrell. One stormy night in 1575, Darrell sent for the midwife Mrs. Barnes, who lived in

a village some distance away. She was offered a large fee to attend a lady in childbirth, but was blindfolded by Darrell's servants so that she would not remember the route to the house.

Arriving at Littlecote, Mrs. Barnes was led upstairs by the master of the house to a richly furnished bedchamber where she found a woman in labor, wearing a mask. Darrell told the midwife that if the woman were delivered safely, she would be handsomely rewarded, but that if the woman died, she herself would lose her life. The terrified midwife did her work, and soon the lady gave birth to a son. When Mrs. Barnes showed the baby to Darrell, he led her to a fireplace on the landing and commanded her to throw the child into the fire. On her knees the distraught woman begged him to let her keep the child herself, but Darrell snatched the baby from her and hurled it into the flames. In the morning Mrs. Barnes was blindfolded again and returned to her home.

While she had awaited the baby's birth, however, Mrs. Barnes had stealthily cut a piece of cloth from the bed curtains and sewn them up again. With this scrap of evidence and her description of the house, she went to the local magistrates, who were able to identify the house as Littlecote. Because of his wealth and influence, however, Darrell was able to escape justice by bribing the judge.

Ultimately another kind of justice dealt with Will Darrell, for one day when he was riding to hounds, he was thrown from his horse and his neck was broken. According to legend the place where he fell was haunted by the image of a child en-

Above: Bosworth Hall in Leicester-shire is the scene of several supernatural phenomena. One of them is the ghost of Lady Lisgar, a Protestant who married into the Catholic family that has always owned Bosworth. She is supposedly condemned to haunt the place as punishment for not letting a priest enter the house to attend a dying maidservant. The present owner keeps a record of Lady Lisgar's visits, and every Easter she has the rooms blessed by a priest.

Above: this stain on the floor of the chapel room at Bosworth Hall is supposed to be consecrated wine, spilled by a priest 300 years ago. He was secretly celebrating Mass when Cromwell's troops rode up to the door. As he ran to his hiding place, he knocked over the chalice. The ancient stain is still damp.
Left: a portrait of Lady Lisgar, whose specter haunts Bosworth Hall.

veloped in flames—like the innocent baby he had murdered.

Within the house itself, the bedchamber where the unknown
lady gave birth, and the landing where the murder took place
have occasionally echoed with the screams of midwife, mother,
and baby, and some people claim to have seen the figure of the
anguished midwife clutching the child.

Theaters are often reputed to be haunted, and London's
Theatre Royal, Drury Lane—generally called the Drury Lane—
claims to be the most haunted in the world. Built in 1663,
though subsequently altered and largely rebuilt, this theater has
seen not only three centuries of theatrical history, but also
more than its share of psychic phenomena. Seven distinct
phantoms have been reported in it.

One of these is a helpful ghost who seems to have a flair for
comedy. When the American actress Betty Jo Jones was playing
the comic part of Ado Annie in *Oklahoma!* at the Drury Lane
in the 1950s, she was distressed because her lines were not
getting laughs. One night she suddenly felt a pair of firm hands
on her shoulders, urging her toward the front of the stage. The
hands then gently repositioned her arms and even adjusted the
tilt of her head. All this was going on as she delivered her lines—
which, for the first time, got their laughs.

On another occasion, the young singer Doreen Duke was
standing nervously on the stage waiting to audition for a part
in *The King and I*. As her turn came, she felt a friendly pat on
her shoulder. Then an unseen hand slipped into hers and led
her downstage. All through the song the hand held hers, and

Above: theater historian McQueen Pope knew Drury Lane and its ghosts and wrote about them. He saw the Man in Gray several times, and almost seemed able to summon the figure to appear at his will.

Right: a group of Americans on a "Psychic Package Tour" are told Drury Lane's history of hauntings by former manager George Hoare.

she reported later that despite the eeriness of the sensation, she felt strangely confident. She got the part.

The possible identity of this kindly ghost was suggested by the late W. J. "Popie" McQueen Pope, a critic and theater historian who was closely associated with the Drury Lane for many years. The ghost was obviously a kindly soul with an expert knowledge of comedy, stage direction, and singing. In McQueen Pope's opinion it could only be the shade of Joe Grimaldi, the beloved 19th-century clown, whose good-heartedness to fellow performers during life had been legendary.

McQueen Pope himself was often connected with the appearances of Drury Lane's most famous phantom, the Man in Gray. In fact, some psychical researchers have suggested that Popie may have unconsciously served as a catalyst for the ghost.

The Man in Gray hasn't been seen recently, but for more than 200 years—from the early 18th century until about the middle of the 20th—he made numerous appearances. Theatergoers and actors have seen him emerge from a wall at the side of the upper circle, walk around behind the seats, and disappear into the wall on the opposite side. The figure, of more than average height with a strong, good-looking face, wears a long gray cloak, sword, riding boots, powdered wig, and three-cornered hat. He never speaks or makes any sound whatever, and appears not to notice those around him. If his way is barred by a living person, he seems to dissolve and then reappear some distance away on the other side of the person.

Above: the clown Joe Grimaldi, as he appeared at his Farewell Benefit at Drury Lane on June 27, 1828. Grimaldi delighted English audiences for many years, and was beloved by his fellow actors. McQueen Pope believed that it was his ghost that once gave Betty Jo Jones (opposite) a gentle push.

Above: the Chateau of Blandy in France, where for many years on the night of All Saints, phantoms were seen flying around the walls, eventually settling on one of the towers. On the same night mysterious cries and the ominous clanking of chains could be heard issuing from a subterranean chamber.

The figure has never been identified, but a clue was uncovered in the late 1840s. While making structural alterations to the theater, some workmen discovered an alcove behind the wall from which the ghost emerged, and inside the alcove they found the skeleton of a man with a dagger between his ribs. A few blackened shreds of cloth still clung to the remains, but crumbled to dust when they were touched.

The skeleton was removed, an inquest held, and an open verdict returned. It has been suggested—though without supporting evidence—that the body may have been that of a victim of Christopher Rick, known as the "Bad Man of Old Drury," who managed the theater during the reign of Queen Anne. Notorious for his evil temper, Rick might have murdered the man and then bricked up the body in the theater. Because he was continually making alterations to the building, this bit of new masonry and plasterwork would not have aroused much suspicion.

After the inquest, the bones of the anonymous man were given a pauper's funeral in a nearby graveyard. According to the theory that burial in consecrated ground will put a wandering spirit at rest, one might have expected the Man in Gray to appear no more. However, according to the theory that a haunting apparition has nothing to do with a spirit, but is a kind of moving picture left on the scene, there was no reason why the Man in Gray shouldn't continue his visits. And he did.

His appearances became frequent from the mid-1930s until McQueen Pope's death in 1960. During this period he would often appear to visitors being shown around the theater by the historian. Assuming that these people actually saw the figure, was their vision in some way stimulated by that of Popie? As we know, people vary in their ability to perceive psychic phenomena, and perhaps also in their ability to project apparitions to other people. McQueen may have been unusually gifted in both respects, and this may account for the way he almost seemed to be able to summon the ghost to appear. Plenty of people had seen the ghost before Popie's day, however, and on occasions when he was not present. He certainly did not invent the ghost, but did he somehow summon it?

Leaving aside the specters of the tourist-attraction variety, let's consider a haunting that took place a few years ago in a charming and comfortable rectory in the village of Yattendon in Berkshire, England. Part of the house was built in the 18th century, but extensive alterations were made around 1900. One of the two ghosts that haunted the house—a pleasant-faced elderly lady—was sometimes seen to follow the path of a staircase removed during the alterations. This kind of behavior is common to many haunts; a part of a wall through which a ghost habitually disappears, for example, often turns out to be the site of a former doorway.

A detailed account of the haunting at Yattendon Rectory appears in Dennis Bardens' book *Ghosts and Hauntings*. Bardens visited the house some years ago and talked to four people who had seen the ghosts: the Reverend A. B. Farmer, the former Rector; his wife; their daughter; and a Mrs. Barton who had stayed with them for several months. Mrs. Barton saw the younger looking of the two ghosts, and described her as "rather pretty" and dressed in a "silvery gray frock" of 18th-century design. A "light seemed to be shining around her." Both Mrs. Barton and Mrs. Farmer, who had seen the figure on another occasion, noticed that she walked above the level of the floor.

This rather elegant lady was not so frequent a visitor as "Mrs. It," whose appearances, said the rector's wife, were quite a "usual occurrence." The figure varied in its distinctness, sometimes resembling a cloud of dark gray smoke, at other times appearing nearly human. She too was dressed in 18th-century clothing. Her skirt, said Mrs. Farmer, was "of thick, black, watered silk. It has a full round bottom, is very voluminous, and the top part of her is covered by a dark shawl, probably wool, under which she carries a basket or handle— her head is covered by a hat (with cap underneath) which is tied on with ribbon under her chin."

Mrs. It seemed to take an interest in the doings of the family. "During the preparation for my daughter's wedding," said Mrs. Farmer, "she was seen inspecting the wedding presents and the arrangements in the kitchen." Was the ghost really aware of what was going on around her? If so, why did she walk up a stairway that no longer existed? But then, ghosts are obviously not bound by the limitations of our world, and perhaps Mrs. It had had a fondness for the stairway when she lived in the rectory some two centuries ago.

Eventually the Farmers left the house, and a new rector came to live there. The new family was not enthusiastic about spectral visitors, and they asked Mr. Farmer to conduct a service of exorcism. He obliged, and the ladies have not been seen since.

Right: the Governor's Mansion, Richmond, Virginia, which has been haunted by the ghost of a beautiful young woman for some 80 years.

Above: portrait of a high-spirited ghost who frolicked around the home of the Murrays of Sandwich, Massachusetts in the 1880s. The couple were often awakened by her nocturnal revels. They attempted to put an end to the nuisance by throwing boots and shoes at her, but the missiles passed through her. Mrs. Murray finally left home; and after Mr. Murray was knocked down by the ghost one time, he too abandoned the house.

The popular notion that graveyards are apt to be haunted has not been confirmed by psychical research. Traditional stories of picturesquely draped figures, clanking chains, and sepulchral voices issuing from the graves are just that—stories. A phantom is much more likely to appear in the places the person frequented while alive.

There is at least one graveyard, however, that does seem to be haunted—by what exactly no one has yet been able to determine. The cemetary lies on a hill in the Wet Mountain Valley area of Colorado, and its phantoms—whatever they are—appear nearly every night for all to see.

In 1880 the township of Silver Cliff enjoyed a "silver rush." Miners and their families invaded the area, and by the end of the year the town's inhabitants numbered more than 5000. The boom did not last, however, and today Silver Cliff is a ghost town in more ways than one, having a living population of only about 100, slightly less than the town's old graveyard.

The strange phenomena that haunt this graveyard were first seen in 1880, when a group of drunken miners returning to their diggings reported seeing eerie blue lights hovering over each grave. Nor were these lights just a by-product of whiskey— they appeared on other nights to sober observers. Many years later in 1956 the ghost lights were written up in the *Wet Mountain Tribune*, and in 1967 they attracted the attention of the *New York Times*. Hundreds of tourists came to see the uncanny spectacle. Two years later, in an article about Colorado in the *National Geographic*, assistant editor Edward J. Linehan described his first look at the lights.

Linehan drove out to the graveyard accompanied by local resident Bill Kleine. It was dark when they reached the place, and Kleine told Linehan to switch off the headlights. They got out of the car, and Kleine pointed: "There! See them? And over there!"

Linehan saw them—"dim, round spots of blue-white light" glowing above the graves. He stepped forward for a better look at one, but it vanished, then slowly reappeared. He switched on his flashlight and aimed it at one of the lights. The beam of the flashlight revealed only a tombstone. For 15 minutes the men pursued the elusive ghost lights among the graves.

Kleine told Linehan that some people theorized that the lights were caused by the reflections of the town lights of Silver Cliff and nearby Westcliff. Linehan turned to look back at the two small towns in the distance. The tiny clusters of their lights seemed far too faint to produce the effect in the graveyard. What's more, Kleine remarked that both he and his wife had seen the ghost lights "when the fog was so thick you couldn't see the towns at all."

Other theories have been advanced to explain the phenomenon. One is that the ghost lights are caused by radioactive ore; but a Geiger counter test of the whole area revealed no trace of radioactivity. Another says the ghost lights are luminous paint, daubed on the tombs by hoaxers; but no evidence has ever been found to support this charge. Still another theory is that the ghost lights reflect the mercury vapor of the Westcliff streetlights; but there were no mercury vapor lights until recently,

Above: an early 19th-century French stage set design showing spirits rising from their graves. The popular notion that ghosts are likely to be seen in a graveyard is not borne out by psychical research. A haunting ghost usually haunts a place that the person lived in or frequented while he was alive. Only a gravedigger's ghost would be likely to haunt a graveyard.

and once when a power failure shut off every light in town, the graveyard lights still shone.

An entirely different approach to the puzzle has been offered by the anthropologist and folklorist Dale Ferguson. He notes that the Cheyenne and other Plains Indians laid their dead to rest on hilltops "sacred to the spirits." Sometimes a particularly powerful medicine man would feel his own death approaching, walk to the "dead men's hill," and lie down there until his soul was "taken." A number of Indian tales, he says, mention "dancing blue spirits" on such sites.

Among the old-timers of Silver Cliff only one explanation holds good: the blue-white spots are the helmet lamps of long dead miners, still seeking frantically for silver on the hillside.

"No doubt someone, someday, will prove there's nothing at all supernatural in the luminous manifestations of Silver Cliff's cemetery," concludes Linehan. "And I will feel a tinge of disappointment."

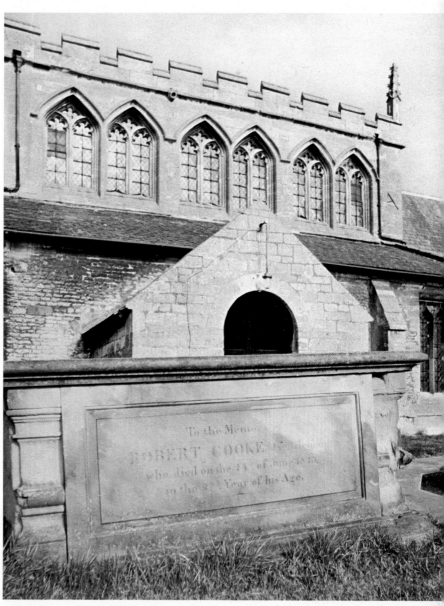

ight: the tomb of a gentleman amed Robert Cooke in Digby, England. The churchyard is haunted y a man on a gray pony, but this henomenon is somewhat banal compared to the whimsical legend surrounding Cooke's grave. It is aid that if one runs 12 times ackward around the tomb, then lisens, one can hear the rattle of aps and saucers in the grave.

4

Ghosts Unhuman

People who assert that ghosts are spirits of the dead—or, as they are sometimes called, "revenants"—are faced with one vexing problem: the supposed revenants almost never appear in the nude. It is conceivable that in the next world we may be clothed in some way, but it seems extremely unlikely that the spirits of people who died in the 18th century, for example, have been provided with knee breeches and wigs. Scientist and writer Lyall Watson puts the problem neatly when he says, "While I am prepared in principle to concede the possibility of an astral body, I cannot bring myself to believe in astral shoes and shirts and hats."

This picture is an illustration for Lewis Carroll's whimsical poem "Phantasmagoria." The creature in the cave is a phantom gaining experience in haunting. According to the poem he is a rather unprepossessing humanlike spirit, but the gloom of the cavern and the imaginations of his victims endow this phantom with beastly ferocity.

54

A.B.FROST.

"A great many apparitions are not human beings at all..."

Below: *Diana the Huntress*, a 16th-century French painting of the Roman goddess (known as Artemis to the Greeks) who is sometimes associated in legend with the Wild Hunt, a ferocious band of hunters and hounds said to ride across the sky at the time of the full moon. One of the most widespread and ancient of European legends, the Wild Hunt is known in France, Germany, and England.

Nor is ghostly clothing the only aspect of the problem. A great many apparitions are not of human beings at all. They include such diverse objects as horse-drawn carriages, ships, motor vehicles, and flitting blue lights. While some people might argue that animals are as likely as humans to have souls, or that the soul might well manifest itself as a blue light, few would credit the motor bus that once haunted a section of London with a spirit of its own.

Many of the most picturesque stories of hauntings concern animals. Few of these are of the domestic pet variety. There is usually something larger than life, and rather sinister, about most spectral beasts. Typical of the breed is England's "Black Shuck," an enormous dog "black as a coal scuttle, big as a donkey, with eyes like saucers." The legend of Shuck appears to have crossed the Atlantic, for the Delaware Valley area of the United States boasts a similar creature called "Black Shep."

The European Wild Hunt also has an American counterpart. Once widespread in Europe, the Wild Hunt myth may have sprung from ancient stories of Diana, goddess of the hunt and of the moon. According to the legend of the Wild Hunt, savage packs of demon dogs driven on by devilish huntsmen are seen riding the sky at full moon. Today the legend remains firmly entrenched in some parts of Europe; the Breton peasants of northwestern France are reluctant to leave their homes at night when the moon is full. An English variation of the legend concerns Herne the Hunter, said to have been Keeper of the King's Deer sometime during the Middle Ages. According to tradition, Herne and his ghostly hounds roam Windsor Forest on the death of a monarch. The American version of the Wild Hunt is the story of Stampede Mesa. Like all folklore it has several variations, one of which was collected and retold by the cattleman-turned-author J. Frank Dobie. His story is set on the Loving Trail in the 1870s, when huge herds of longhorns were driven north from Texas to Kansas. Already the open range was being fenced in by farmers, contemptuously termed "nesters" by the free-riding cowhands, and the bouts of violence that broke out between cattlemen and farmers are part of the history of the West.

On one drive north, a trail boss came across a group of nesters who had begun building fences and stockades right across the trail. They were prepared to fight. When the cattleman drew his pistol, the nesters leveled rifles and shotguns at him. The infuriated cattle boss wheeled his horse and rode to the rear of the herd.

"Move 'em!" he shouted to his men, firing his Colt into the air. Within seconds the cattle were panicked into a stampede, thundering wildly toward the farm settlement. Fences were smashed, wagons overturned, crops trampled. The nesters were crushed to death under the thundering hooves.

When the herd arrived in Abilene, the cattle boss reported the stampede as an accident, and after a brief inquiry the incident was closed. But the truth spread among Texas cowboys and the place where the massacre occurred on the edge of *mesa*, or flat-topped hill, became known as Stampede Mesa. Soon campfire tales included a ghostly sequel to the story. On

Above: Herne the Hunter, the phantom believed to ride through Windsor Forest where the original Herne once served as a keeper.
A malignant spirit, formerly blamed for many misfortunes including cattle diseases, he now foretells the death of the British monarch.

Below: Henry VIII supervising an attempt to lay Herne's ghost by destroying the haunted oak tree where the man had hanged himself after being convicted of a crime, possibly poaching or witchcraft.

moonlit nights, it was said, a phantom herd could be seen crashing over the ground, the dying screams of the farmers mingling with the rumble of hooves and the crack of gunfire.

Shortly after Dobie's written account of Stampede Mesa appeared in print, a popular song, "Ghost Riders in the Sky" further immortalized the story in the words:

". . . . and all at once a mighty herd of red-eyed cows he saw, A-ploughin' through the rugged sky, and up a cloudy draw . . ."

While many stories of animal apparitions conform to some such standard folklore pattern, there are some striking exceptions. There is something terrifyingly individual, for instance, about the black cat of Killakee. From 1968 until the early 70s, intense poltergeist activity (the movement of objects by an unseen force) occurred in Killakee House in County Dublin, Ireland. Despite exorcism and the investigations of psychical researchers these phenomena continue sporadically today. Killakee is now an Arts Center, where Irish artists paint, sculpt, and display their work. It is owned by Mrs. Margaret O'Brien, who bought the house in the late 1960s and had some alterations made on it.

For years stories had circulated locally of a large cat, the size of an Airedale dog, that haunted the overgrown gardens of the house—"haunted" because the tales covered a period of 40 or 50 years, much longer than the life span of a normal animal. Early in 1968 Mrs. O'Brien herself caught fleeting glimpses of a big black animal that would disappear into the shrubbery.

At the time two local men and Tom McAssey, an artist friend of Mrs. O'Brien's, were at work in the house, redecorating the

Below: ruins of the Hell Fire Club on Montpellier Hill above Killakee House. Once a local farmer and a clergyman went up to investigate the notorious activities, for they believed the Club had murdered a young visitor to the neighborhood. They were admitted to a banquet seemingly presided over by a large black cat. The priest threw holy water at the cat, pandemonium broke out, and the place caught fire and burned down.

ballroom and the stone-flagged hall. One dark night in March, they were just finishing the day's work in the hall when something peculiar happened. McAssey's account follows: "I had just locked the heavy front door, pushing a six-inch bolt into its socket. Suddenly one of the two men with me said that the door had opened again. We turned, startled. The lock was good and the bolt was strong . . . and both fastened on the inside.

"We peered into the shadowed hallway, and then I walked forward, and sure enough the door stood wide open, letting in a cold breeze. Outside in the darkness I could just discern a black-draped figure, but could not see its face. I thought someone was playing a trick and said 'Come in. I see you.' A low gutteral voice answered: 'You can't see me. Leave this door open.'

"The men standing directly behind me both heard the voice, but thought it spoke in a foreign language. They ran. A long drawn snore came from the shadow, and in panic I slammed the heavy door and ran too. Halfway across the gallery I turned and looked back. The door was again open and a monstrous black cat crouched in the hall, its red-flecked amber eyes fixed on me."

Val McGann, the former Irish pole-vault champion who also paints and shows his work at Killakee, was not in the least surprised by McAssey's story. He lives in a cottage in the woods nearby, and on several occasions has seen a similar cat. "The first time it frightened me stiff, but on subsequent occasions I have been more amazed at the sight of it. It is about the size of a biggish dog, with terrible eyes. I've even stalked it with my shotgun, but have never been able to corner it."

Behind Killakee House looms Montpellier Hill, a steep bare mount surmounted by the ruin of what was once a hunting

Above: the tomb of Lord Byron's dog Boatswain at Newstead Abbey, the Byrons' ancestral home. The poet buried his dog on the site where the high altar had stood in the days when Newstead was a real abbey. A phantom hound is said to haunt the place—as does the Goblin Friar, who brings bad news. Below: La Grand Bête, a phantom bull of French folklore, may be related to the spectral and mythical bulls venerated by the Celts.

lodge. This is known locally as the Hell Fire Club, and there is some evidence that in the 18th century it was used by the young rakes of Dublin for orgies. Tradition holds that the Devil burned it down—rather ungratefully—during a Black Mass. Another story connected with the place says that a huge black cat was enthroned there during orgies to symbolize Satan when he did not turn up in person. The specter of this cat, say the locals, is the thing that haunts Killakee Arts Center.

Not far from Killakee lies the township of Rathfarnham, the haunt, it is said, of another unhuman ghost: a black coach driven by a headless coachman. This is a variation on a theme which, like black dogs and wild hunts, recurs in both Britain and the United States. A similar coach was said to hurtle over Boston's Beacon Hill in the 19th century, and the famous Deadwood stage was reported rumbling along its old route in North Dakota decades after it had made its last run.

Unfortunately for the romantics, historians have a plausible explanation for these phantom coaches. In both America and Britain, fresh corpses for dissection in the medical schools were hard to come by until the early 19th century. At that time various "anatomy laws" were passed permitting doctors to experiment on the bodies of dead paupers and vagrants. Until then graverobbers, variously known as "ghouls" and "resurrection men," did a brisk trade in newly buried corpses. To transport a body was obviously difficult without being spotted, and the penalties for grave robbing were high. So the ghouls transported their grisly wares in black coaches after first spreading frightening tales of ghostly conveyances throughout the neighborhood.

No such simple explanation was forthcoming when, in the mid-1930s, a modern version of the phantom coach began to plague London's Kensington area. The junction of St. Mark's Road and Cambridge Gardens had long been considered dangerous because of the sharp corner, and to add to the danger the big red buses on the Number 7 route turned into Cambridge Gardens at that point. Hundreds of minor accidents—and several fatal ones—took place there before the local authority finally straightened out the bend.

The decision to do so was partly influenced by a spate of reports from late night motorists. They said they had crashed at the spot after swerving to avoid a careering double-deck bus that traveled silently down St. Mark's Road in the middle of the night—when no buses were in service.

One report read: "I was turning the corner and saw a bus tearing towards me. The lights of the top and bottom deck, and the headlights, were full on but I could see no sign of crew or passengers. I yanked my steering wheel hard over, and mounted the pavement [sidewalk], scraping the roadside wall. The bus just vanished."

This report was typical. The local coroner discovered more evidence while conducting an inquest on a driver who had hit the wall head on, rather than merely scraping it. An eye witness said that the phantom bus had suddenly appeared, speeding toward the car the second before the driver made his fatal swerve. When the coroner expressed doubt, dozens of

Above: Fred Archer, a famous British jockey who died in 1886 at the age of 29, is reputed to haunt the track at Newmarket in Suffolk. The sight of his ghost on a phantom horse is supposed to have occasionally caused live horses to shy or stumble during a race.

Right: this 19th-century Japanese print shows an apparition of a monstrous cat terrorizing some courtiers. The picture may be based on the story of "The Vampire Cat of Nabeshima," in which a huge spectral cat kills the prince's favorite mistress, then assumes the lady's form and torments the prince until he falls ill. Eventually the true identity of the beautiful woman is discovered, and in a struggle with the guard who guessed her secret she reverts to feline form.

residents offered to testify that they had seen the apparition. Among the volunteer witnesses was an official from a nearby bus depot who said he had seen the vehicle draw silently up outside the depot in the small hours, and then disappear.

The mystery was never solved, but it may be significant that after the road alterations were made the bus was not seen again. Had it somehow been projected onto the scene to dramatize the danger inherent in the intersection? If so, it was a rather drastic measure—and on the part of whom? A more likely explanation is that it was a visible form of the apprehen-

Many tales of phantom coaches were deliberately spread by grave robbers to deflect suspicion of their own real coaches as they pursued their nocturnal and illegal missions to and from graveyards. Above: *The Student Recognizing His Mother* is a typically melodramatic Victorian engraving of a potential—though unlikely—hazard attached to the practice of robbing graves to obtain bodies for dissection. The medical student, supervising two grave robbers, is horrified to discover that the body is that of his own mother. Right: a "resurrectionist" is interrupted by an outraged ghost.

sions of the motorists themselves, who expected danger at that point. This theory, however, doesn't account for the visions of the bus depot official and other bystanders. The phantom bus will probably remain an unsolved puzzle.

Considering the essential loneliness of life at sea and the many strange natural phenomena of the oceans, it's not surprising that sailors—a notoriously superstitious lot—have created and perpetuated stories of phantom ships. The best-known of these stories is the legend of the Flying Dutchman.

"Once upon a time, a good many years ago, there was a ship's captain who feared neither God nor his Saints. He is said to have been a Dutchman, but I do not know, nor does it greatly matter, from which town he came. . . ."

This leisurely opening comes from one of August Jal's *Scenes of Maritime Life* published in 1832. Jal was launching his own version of a story that had been current for at least a hundred years before he put pen to paper, and that achieved immortality a few years later in Richard Wagner's opera *Der fliegende Holländer (The Flying Dutchman)*. It concerned an impious captain, doomed for eternity to sail his ghostly ship around the Cape of Good Hope, an ill omen to other mariners.

According to Jal's version, the captain was making a passage around Good Hope when he ran into a head wind "strong enough to blow the horns off a bull." The ship was soon in grave danger, and the crew implored the captain to turn back but, either mad or drunk, he "proceeded to sing songs of a horrible and blasphemous nature," finally retiring to his cabin to smoke his pipe and drink beer. As the ship began to disintegrate, the captain went further and began to challenge the Almighty "with fearful oaths" to sink him.

"But even as he did so, the clouds opened and a Form alighted on the quarter-deck of the ship. This Form is said to have been the Almighty Himself. The crew and passengers were stricken with fear, but the Captain went on smoking his pipe, and did not even touch his cap when the Form addressed him. . ."

After bandying words with the Form and shooting at it with a pistol, the captain received his sentence: he was "accursed" and condemned to sail forever without rest.

"'Gall,' said the Form, 'shall be your drink and red hot iron your meat. Of your crew only a cabin boy shall remain with you; horns shall grow out of his forehead, and he shall have the muzzle of a tiger and a skin rougher than that of a dogfish. And since it is your delight to torment sailors, you shall torment them. For you shall be the evil spirit of the sea, and your ship shall bring misfortune to all who sight it.'"

"'Amen to that!' laughed the captain, unabashed."

Jal goes on to record how the story spread among seagoing men, and how the ways of the Flying Dutchman—a term applied to both the captain and his ship—became notorious. The Dutchman cast other ships away on uncharted shoals, becalmed them and then jeered at their distress, turned their wine and water sour and all their food to beans. Occasionally he would draw alongside a vessel and send letters aboard; if the letters were read the ship was lost. Sometimes an empty boat

The Coach that Wasn't There

One night in August 1878 Major W. went to the front door of his house in an isolated part of Scotland for a breath of air before going to bed. As he stood looking out, he saw a coach and pair coming up his drive. Two men were sitting on the coachman's box. They drove swiftly up the drive and over the lawn toward a stream, oblivious of the Major's warning shout about the water beyond. Then they wheeled sharply and drove back.

By this time Major W.'s son had joined him with a lantern, and the boy was able to catch a glimpse of the carriage's occupant. It was a stiff-looking figure, probably a woman, draped in white from head to toe. This person gave no sign of recognition, nor did the coachman and his companion. The Major did not recognize his visitors or their carriage, which he found odd because he knew the neighborhood well. The coach left as it had come.

The following day Major W. made inquiries, but no one had heard of or seen the mysterious coach — no one except the Major, his son, and his wife and daughter who had been drawn to the window by his shout. They examined the ground over which the coach had driven. It was soft and damp, but bore no trace of wheels or hooves.

would be seen to draw alongside the *Flying Dutchman*—a sure sign of death to the watchers. Perhaps worst of all, the ghost ship could change its appearance so that it was impossible to recognize it until too late. According to some stories, though, the wicked captain had repented, and could be seen standing on his devastated quarter-deck, bareheaded, crying to God for mercy while a crew of skeletal figures tied on more sail.

Whether or not Jal realized it, there was a "flying Dutchman" of sorts, an historical character. His name was Captain Bernard Fokke. He was born in The Hague in the early 17th century, and became the master of a ship called a Dutch East Indiaman. Little is known of his personal life, but he was renowned among British and French seamen as well as his own countrymen for his skilled seamanship, and for his constant experiments with his vessel's rigging. By strengthening the masts with iron sheathing and making innovations to the sail plan—some of which were to influence the building of China tea clippers 200 years later—Fokke was able to make surprisingly swift passages to India. When his ship vanished mysteriously, rumors circulated that he had made a pact with the Devil to ensure his success, and that the Devil had claimed him. The mysterious Captain Fokke may have inspired the legend of the Flying Dutchman.

Another ghost ship, familiar to people who live on the southern coast of New England, is the flaming hulk of the *Palatine*. In 1752 the *Palatine* set sail from Holland, bound for Philadelphia and carrying would-be colonists. The voyage took place in the depths of winter, and as the *Palatine* neared the coast of New England, foul weather blew her badly off course. To make matters worse, there was mutiny. The captain fell, or was pushed, overboard, and the crew robbed the passengers before leaving the ship and its occupants to their fate.

About 11 miles off the coast of Long Island between Montauk and Gay Head lies the windswept, desolate stretch of land called Block Island. It was here, one morning between Christmas and New Year, that the battered *Palatine* finally grounded. Block Island was the home of a poor community of fishermen, who were said to eke out their livelihood by causing shipwrecks and then plundering the grounded vessels. On this occasion, though, they showed mercy, and managed to save the passengers before looting the wreck, setting it on fire, and leaving it to drift back out to sea and sink.

By a tragic oversight, however, they had missed one woman who, demented by the storms and violence, had hidden herself aboard. As the burning hulk was swept seaward by the tide the onlookers were horrified to see her standing on deck screaming for help. By that time there was nothing they could do.

Ever since then the people living along the Rhode Island coast opposite Block Island have watched at Christmastime for the fiery outline of a ship which appears on the water near the spot where the *Palatine* foundered. The phenomenon is sporadic, but reports of sighting "a great red fireball on the ocean" appeared as recently as 1969.

It may be that the Palatine Light, as it is called, is a natural phenomenon—some kind of electrical discharge such as St. Elmo's fire. If so, however, we're still left with the perplexing

Above: a scene from a 19th-century production of Wagner's opera *The Flying Dutchman*, one of several versions of the legend of the cursed phantom ship. The captain is condemned to sail forever unless he can find a woman willing to sacrifice everything for his sake. In the opera the curse is lifted by a Norwegian girl, Senta.

Left: a painting of the *Flying Dutchman* appearing in the sky near the Cape of Good Hope. The sight of the ghostly ship was considered an ill omen by sailors, and it was supposed to have the power to lead ships astray. The waters off the Cape are known for mirages, and this may account for sightings of the *Dutchman*.

fact that it occurs only during Christmas week, and that it has done so, off and on, for more than 200 years.

The seas, it would appear, are almost as crowded with phantom ships as the country roads of England are with phantom coaches. Captain Kidd's ship is reported to sail the coves of New England, checking on the pirate's legendary treasure. Another pirate ship, that of Jean Lafitte, has appeared in the harbor of Galveston, Texas, where it was supposedly sunk during the 1820s. A 19th-century Baltimore clipper named the *Dash*, which vanished at sea, allegedly revisited its home port periodically when any relative of a crew member died.

During World War II a U.S. frigate cleared for action after sighting two unidentified vessels approaching it off the California coast. The skipper was both baffled and embarrassed when the ships suddenly vanished, and his radar showed no sign of any vessels in the area whatsoever.

Visions of ships can often be explained away as a combination of atmospheric conditions and the state of mind of the percipient. In the old days the length of sea voyages and the dangers that attended them would inevitably have made some sailors overly prone to seeing things. Modern sea voyages are short and safe, but sailors at war, tense and prepared to sight an enemy ship, might see what they were expecting—without its necessarily being there.

It's somewhat more difficult to account for what a Miss Wynne saw one gray afternoon in autumn 1926 while out for a walk. At that time, Miss Wynne had recently moved to a village near Bury St. Edmonds in Suffolk, England, and she often took walks in the afternoon to explore the countryside. On this particular day she and a companion, Miss Allington, set out through the fields to see the church of the neighboring village, Bradfield St. George. Here is her account of the experience, given in Sir Ernest Bennett's *Apparitions and Haunted Houses*:

"In order to reach the church, which we could see plainly ahead of us to the right, we had to pass through a farmyard, whence we came out onto a road. We had never previously taken this particular walk, nor did we know anything about the topography of the hamlet of Bradfield St. George. Exactly opposite us on the further side of the road and flanking it, we saw a high wall of greenish-yellow bricks. The road ran past us for a few yards, then curved away from us to the left. We walked along the road, following the brick wall round the bend, where we came upon tall, wrought-iron gates set in the wall. I think the gates were shut, or one side may have been open. The wall continued on from the gates and disappeared round the curve of the road. Behind the wall, and towering above it, was a cluster of tall trees. From the gates a drive led away among these trees to what was evidently a large house. We could just see a corner of the roof above a stucco front, in which I remember noticing some windows of Georgian design. The rest of the house was hidden by the branches of the trees. We stood by the gates for a moment, speculating as to who lived [there]."

It was not until four or five months later that Miss Wynne and Miss Allington took that walk again. "We walked up through the farmyard as before, and out onto the road, where, suddenly, we both stopped dead of one accord and gasped. 'Where's the wall?' we queried simultaneously. It was not there. The road was flanked by nothing but a ditch, and beyond the ditch lay a wilderness of tumbled earth, weeds, mounds, all overgrown with the trees which we had seen on our first visit. We followed the road round the bend, but there were no gates, no drive, no corner of a house to be seen. We were both very puzzled. At first we thought that our house and wall had been pulled down since our last visit, but closer inspection showed a pond and other small pools amongst the mounds where the house had been visible. It was obvious that they had been there a long time."

Inquiries revealed that no one in the area had ever heard of the house. Only the two women seem to have seen it (Miss Allington corroborated Miss Wynne's report). If it was an hallucination it is certainly an hallucination on a grand scale. What psychic force brought it into existence? Did some buried memory of such a house in such a situation exist in the mind of Miss Wynne or Miss Allington— a memory that one of them subconsciously wanted to visualize, and was able not only to visualize but also to project so that her companion saw it too? Or, to consider an even more fantastic idea, were they somehow transported back or forward in time so that their own lives for a few moments coincided with the actual existence of the house?

Clearly, an apparition such as this, observed by two people in broad daylight raises some intriguing questions about the nature of humans and about the nature of the world we see.

Above: the Palatine Light. More than 200 years after it was set on fire, the ship *Palatine* is still seen sporadically, but only at Christmastime, off Block Island, N.Y.

Right: Okehampton Castle in Devonshire. One of the more sinister of England's many phantom coaches is said to follow the old road between Tavistock and Okehampton. It is constructed of human bones— those of the four husbands of the wicked Lady Howard, whose pale and sheeted specter rides inside it. A skeleton hound runs before her, and according to the legend, his task is to pluck each night a blade of grass from Okehampton Park to take back to Fitzford, the lady's family home. This penance for her supposed murder of her husbands is to continue until every blade of grass is plucked—that is, until the end of the world itself.

Above: a Spitfire, most famous aircraft of the Royal Air Force in World War II. People who live near Biggin Hill Airfield claim that one of these planes, piloted by a flyer who never returned from his mission, has been heard screaming in to land. Some report seeing the plane, and say that the pilot signals his return with a low victory roll, a sideways flip, announcing a successful mission.

69

5

Family Ghosts

"It started low at first like, then it mounted up into a crescendo; there was definitely some human element in the voice . . . the door to the bakery where I worked was open too, and the men stopped to listen. Well, it rose as I told you to a crescendo, and you could almost make out one or two Gaelic words in it; then gradually it went away slowly. Well, we talked about it for a few minutes and at last, coming on to morning, about five o'clock, one of the bread servers came in and he says to me, 'I'm afraid they'll need you to take out the cart, for I just got word of the death of an aunt of mine.' It was at his cart that the bansidhe had keened."

The Screaming Skull of Bettiscombe Manor, long supposed to be that of a West Indian slave taken to England in the 18th century, is shown here beneath a portrait of John Pinney, the landowner who brought the slave to Bettiscombe. The skull is alleged to scream if it is removed from its home, a characteristic shared by other family skulls found both in Britain and in the United States.

"The banshee was permitted to howl out its sorrow"

More commonly spelled "banshee," as it is pronounced, "bansidhe" is the Gaelic word for "fairy woman," a creature whose mournful cry is said to foretell death. The above quotation was taken from a British Broadcasting Corporation program that Irish psychical researcher Sheila St. Clair conducted with several people who claimed to have themselves experienced the hideous wail of the banshee. In the same program an elderly man from County Down described the fairy death wail in more detail. "It was a mournful sound" he said; "it would have put ye in mind of them ould yard cats on the wall, but it wasn't cats, I know it meself; I thought it was a bird in torment or something . . . a mournful cry it was, and then it was going a wee bit further back, and further until it died away altogether . . ."

The banshee cried for ancient Irish heroes. It wailed for King Connor McNessa, Fin McCool, and the great Brian Boru, whose victory over the Danes in 1014 ended their sovereignty over Ireland. More recently its eerie voice is said to have echoed in the Cork village of Sam's Cross when General Michael Collins, commander-in-chief of the Irish Free State Army, was killed in an ambush near there in 1922. A few months later when Commandant Sean Dalton was shot in Tralee, a song recalls: "When Dalton died sure the bansidhe cried, in the Valley of Knockanure."

Although its name translates as "fairy woman," most authorities define the banshee as a spirit rather than a fairy. In some families—the O'Briens, for example—the banshee is considered to be almost a guardian angel, silently watching over the fortunes of the family and guiding its members along safe and profitable paths. When an O'Brien dies this guardian performs her last service, keening for the departing soul.

A County Antrim man gave his interpretation of the banshee to Sheila St. Clair. He claimed that the Irish, as a reward for their piety, had been blessed with guardian spirits to take care of their individual clans. Because these celestial beings were not normally able to express themselves in human terms and yet became involved with the family under their care, God allowed them to show their deep feeling only when one of their charges died. Then the banshee was permitted to howl out its sorrow.

James O'Barry was the pseudonym used by a Boston businessman who wrote to the author on the subject, and if O'Barry's testimony is to be believed the banshee, like some other creatures of European folklore, has crossed the Atlantic.

Like many of Boston's Irish Catholics, O'Barry is descended from a family that arrived in Massachusetts in 1848, fleeing the great famine that decimated Ireland's population in the 19th century. His great-great grandfather started a small grocery business, and today O'Barry and his two brothers run a supermarket chain which has branches throughout New England.

"When I was a very small boy," O'Barry recalls, "I was lying in bed one morning when I heard a weird noise, like a demented woman crying. It was spring, and outside the window the birds were singing, the sun was shining, and the sky was blue. I thought for a moment or two that a wind had sprung up, but a glance at the barely stirring trees told me that this was not so.

"I got up, dressed, and went downstairs, and there was my

Above: a banshee warns a man of approaching death in his family. Normally heard rather than seen, the banshee wails whenever a member of the family she watches over is about to die. Many Irish and Scottish Highland families claim to have such guardian spirits.

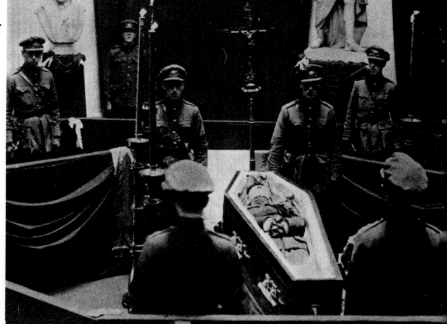

Right: the body of the Irish revolutionary leader Michael Collins lying in state in Dublin in 1922. The voice of the banshee is said to have keened in the village of Sam's Cross, County Cork, when Collins died there in an ambush.

father sitting at the kitchen table with tears in his eyes. I had never seen him weep before. My mother told me that they had just heard, by telephone, that my grandfather had died in New York. Although he was an old man, he was fit as a fiddle, and his death was unexpected."

It was some years before O'Barry learned the legend of the banshee, and he then recalled the wailing noise he had heard on the death of his grandfather. In 1946 he was to hear it for the second time. In May of that year he was an administrative officer serving with the U.S. Air Force in the Far East. One morning at six o'clock he was awakened by a low howl.

"That time," he said, "I was instantly aware of what it was. I sat bolt upright in my bed, and the hair on the back of my neck prickled. The noise got louder, rising and falling like an air-raid siren. Then it died away, and I realized that I was terribly depressed. I knew my father was dead. A few days later I had notification that this was so."

Seventeen years later, O'Barry heard the hair-stiffening voice of the banshee a third time. He was in Toronto, Canada, by himself, enjoying a combined holiday and business trip.

"Again I was in bed, reading the morning papers," he said, "when the dreadful noise was suddenly filling my ears. I thought of my wife, my young son, my two brothers, and I thought 'Good God, don't let it be one of them.' But for some reason I knew it wasn't."

The date was November 22, 1963, the time shortly after noon, and the Irish banshee was bewailing the death of an acquaintance of O'Barry's—John F. Kennedy, President of the United States.

The banshee is rarely seen as an apparition, but when she does appear she takes the form of a red-haired, green-eyed woman. The Welsh have their own harbinger of death, a revolting old woman known as "The Dribbling Hag." In Scotland, "death women" can sometimes be seen on the banks of westward-running streams, washing the clothing of those about to die. One Scottish family, the Ewens of the Isle of Mull, Argyllshire, preserve a curious legend concerning their own death spirit. In the early 16th century Eoghan a' Chin Bhig—Ewen of the Little Head—lived at Loch Sguabain Castle, Isle of Mull, as clan chief. His wife was the daughter of another chief, The MacLaine, and Ewen and his father-in-law were forever quarreling. In 1538 matters reached serious proportions, and both sides collected followers for a showdown.

The evening before the battle, Ewen was walking near Loch Sguabain when he came across an old woman washing a bundle of blood-stained shirts in a stream. She was dressed from head to foot in green and Ewen knew that she was a death woman, and that the shirts were those of the men who would die in the morning. He asked if his own shirt was among them, and she said that it was. "But," she added, "if your wife offers you bread and cheese with her own hand, without you asking for it, you will be victorious."

As dawn broke and Ewen buckled on his sword he waited anxiously for his wife to offer him the food. She failed to do so. Demoralized, Ewen led his followers to defeat at the hands of the MacLaines. At the height of the battle a swinging ax cut off his

Above: Cortachy Castle in Aberdeenshire, Scotland, the home of the Ogilvys, Earls of Airlie since 1641. An approaching death among the Ogilvys is signalled by the sound of ghostly drumming outside the castle walls. According to legend, a handsome young drummer was once caught in a compromising position with a Lady Airlie. As punishment, he was sealed in his own drum and hurled from the highest tower of the castle.

head clean from his shoulders. His black horse galloped away, its headless rider still sitting upright in the saddle. From that day onward, the dead chief himself became his clan's death warning, for when a Ewen was to die the phantom horse and headless rider were seen and heard thundering down Glen More on the shores of Loch Sguabain.

Three members of the Ewen family within living memory have reported seeing the phantom. At Lochbuie, home of the present clan chief, the vision is said to herald serious illness in the family as well as death itself.

Sheila St. Clair offers a theory to account for the banshee. In her book *Psychic Phenomena in Ireland* she says: "I would suggest that just as we inherit physical characteristics—for instance red hair, blue eyes—we also inherit memory cells, and that those of us with strong tribal lineages riddled with inter-

Above: England's Brown Lady of Raynham Hall is one of the few specters ever to be caught by the camera—or partially caught, anyway. The photographer, who had come to Raynham to photograph its staircase one day in September 1936, saw only this transparent figure. Earlier manifestations of the Brown Lady were better defined. She was said to wear a coif and a brocade gown, and to have empty eye sockets. According to one legend, the appearance of the lady heralds a death among the family owning the house.

marriage have the 'bansidhe' as part of an inherited memory. The symbolic form of a weeping woman may well be stamped on our racial consciousness. Ireland's women are experts at weeping over their slain sons and daughters. And just as our other levels of consciousness are not answerable to the limitations of time in our conscious mind, so a particular part of the mind throws up a symbolic hereditary pattern that has in the past been associated with tragedy in the tribe, be it woman, hare, or bird, as a kind of subliminal 'four-minute warning' so that we may prepare ourselves for that tragedy."

Essentially this theory agrees with psychiatrist C. G. Jung's theory of the "collective unconscious," an inherited storehouse of memories of mankind's early experiences.

The inherited memory theory—which might be applied to other family death warnings as well—is a fairly comfortable one compared to the belief, held by many of these families, that the warning represents a curse on their lives.

Mrs. Mary Balfour, an octagenarian who has outlived most of her noble Scottish family, believes her clan spirit, a phantom piper, to be the result of a curse.

Below: Glamis Castle in Scotland, the ancestral home of the Bowes-Lyon family, is as likely a place for a ghost as can be imagined. A specter of a 16th-century Lady Glamis is said to haunt the clock tower, but she is quite eclipsed by the legendary "horror" of Glamis, a secret known only to the head of the family. This has not stopped outsiders from speculating as to its nature. One theory is that a secret room in the castle contains skeletons of members of another clan who, centuries ago, were locked in the room by the earl and left to starve to death. Right: Duncan's Hall, one of the castle's 100-odd rooms, is named for the king murdered in Shakespeare's *Macbeth*, but the real Duncan never visited the castle.

Above: this portrait of the Third Earl of Strathmore and his family hangs in the drawing room at Glamis. The small, slightly distorted boy in the picture feeds the legend that the secret of Glamis is a "monster child" born to the Bowes-Lyons and hidden in the castle.

Above: Sandford Orcas Manor is haunted by seven ghosts.

Below: Sawston Hall, Cambridgeshire, is reputedly haunted by the Queen nicknamed "Bloody Mary" for her persecution of the Protestants in the 16th century. But if Mary does visit Sawston, it is as a friend, for its owner gave her shelter when, before becoming queen, she was in danger. Above right: the Tapestry Room at Sawston, where Mary spent the night and supposedly still appears.

"According to tradition the curse was laid by a dying man, fatally wounded by one of my forebears in a clan feud. He said that from then onward our family should know of a death in their ranks two or three days before it took place. As the death would be inevitable, it was a kind of torture. Over the years it has been a torture to me; I've heard the piper, who plays a lament on the Great Pipes, in Edinburgh, on the Isle of Skye, on trains, and in my own flat in Berkeley Square, London.

"So far I have never seen him. On occasion I have been relieved to turn around when the music sounded and see a street piper, such as used to be common in Edinburgh and Glasgow years ago. At such times I knew that no warning was intended. I first heard the lament as a girl of two or three in Inverness, and I know that when I last hear it, it will be calling me."

Other eminent families are afflicted with different kinds of ghosts. Perhaps the most haunted family in Britain is that of the Bowes-Lyons, Earls of Strathmore, the family of the present queen's mother. Their ancestral home, Glamis Castle in County Angus, was the setting of Shakespeare's *Macbeth*—although King Duncan may not have even visited the castle, let alone been murdered there. Glamis (pronounced "Glahms") was, however, the place where King Malcolm II was stabbed to death in the 11th century. A stain said to have been caused by his blood still marks the floor in one of the castle's myriad rooms. Several ghosts haunt Glamis—a little black boy, a lady in gray, a former earl who supposedly played cards with the Devil and lost. But the most celebrated—and chilling—of all the castle's legends is the "Horror" of Glamis.

No one outside the Strathmore family knows what form the Horror takes, but evidence suggests that it is not merely an old wives' tale, and that some terrible mystery does lurk within the grim stone walls. The most frequent story is that a monster child was born to the Strathmores, so hideous that to look upon it was to invite madness. The thing lived to an unnaturally old age—and some say that it still lives locked away in a hidden room.

The possible existence of a hidden room in which the monster could be kept intrigued a party of house guests at Glamis some years ago, and they organized a search for it. Methodically the guests hung a piece of linen from every window they could find. When they went outside, they discovered that over a dozen windows were unaccounted for. The then-Lord Strathmore, who had been away during the experiment, returned unexpectedly and, realizing what his guests had been up to, flew into an uncharacteristically furious temper.

It was he who some years later told a friend who asked about the Horror: "If you could know of it, you would thank God you were not me."

Another theory about the Glamis Horror is presented by Eric Maple in his book *The Realm of Ghosts*. According to Maple, centuries ago during a clan feud some members of the Ogilvie Clan fleeing from the Lindsays, sought refuge at Glamis. The Earl of Strathmore was bound by the laws of hospitality to admit them, but not wishing to appear partisan he took them to a remote room of the castle, locked them in, and left them to starve. Many years after they had died, their screams continued to echo occasionally in that part of the castle. Eventually one earl decided to investigate, and he made his way to the room from which the noises seemed to come. On opening the door and glimpsing the scene within, he fell backward in a faint into the arms of his companion. The earl refused to tell anyone what he had seen, but he had the door to the room bricked up. "There is a tradition," writes Maple, "that the spectacle within the haunted room was unbelievably horrible, for some of the starving men had actually died in the act of gnawing the flesh from their arms."

Above: Lady Louisa Carteret, who is supposed to haunt Longleat, the home of the Marquess of Bath. Below: the passageway at Longleat where, according to legend, Lady Louisa's husband and her lover fought a duel, ending in the lover's death. The apparition of the lady has been seen, and feelings of terror experienced here.

Both this story and the monster child story may be mere speculation. The truth of the matter is known only to the Earl of Strathmore. Tradition has it that each Strathmore heir is told the secret by his father on his 21st birthday. Lady Granville, a member of the Bowes-Lyon family, told ghost hunter J. Wentworth Day that female members of the family are never let in on the mystery. "We were never allowed to talk about it when we were children," she said. "My father and grandfather refused absolutely to discuss it."

There, as far as outsiders are concerned, the matter rests.

Some less prominent families have a more tangible form of ancestral Horror. Skulls kept as guardians and treated with a mixture of awe and affection were almost a fashion at one time, according to Celtic folklore—and again the custom seems to have crossed the Atlantic to America. The late A. J. Pew, a journalist from California, told the author of his family's own skull.

Pew's family was French, and arrived in the Louisiana Territory during the late 17th century. Family records from the earliest days of their settlement told of a skull, supposedly that of an ancestor who had been burned as a heretic in the Middle Ages, which was kept in a carved wooden box.

Like other such cranial family heirlooms, the skull—affectionately called "Ferdinand" by the Pews—showed an apparent sensitivity to its surroundings. "It had to be kept in the family house," wrote Pew, "and if it was taken off the premises it screamed. If it screamed *indoors*, it meant a death among us."

Apparently, however, Pew's father suspected the story to be a myth. He had the skull examined by a surgeon, who stated that in his opinion it had all the characteristics of an Indian skull, possibly one from the Florida area.

Below: a kind of "still life with death" including the Screaming Skull of Bettiscombe Manor. Here serving as an ornament of sorts, the skull was also at one time used as a toy by the children of a tenant of Bettiscombe; and local villagers even maintain that unidentified persons or phantoms simply called "them" bowled with it.

Above: Burton Agnes Hall in Yorkshire houses the skull of Anne Griffith, who built it. Shortly after it was finished, Anne was attacked by robbers while out walking, and mortally wounded. On her deathbed she asked her sisters to keep her head within the Hall, but they failed to keep the promise. Frightful noises broke out in the house—stamping footsteps, crashing doors—and a few weeks later the intimidated sisters had Anne's skull restored to her home.

"I've rather lost touch with the relic and the branch of the family who owned it," Pew said, "but from that evidence I would guess that it came into the hands of the Pew family after their arrival in America, not before. Possibly some ancestor wanted to establish himself in this country, and cooked up the skull story to add an air of mystery to himself. Certainly my father never found concrete evidence of the skull actually screaming—only people who remembered people who had heard it scream."

The Pew family skull is not the only one of its kind. Several English families have possessed—sometimes reluctantly—bony relics that resist any attempts to give them a decent burial.

Burton Agnes Hall, a beautifully restored Elizabethan house, was for many years haunted by the apparition of Anne Griffith, the daughter of Sir Henry Griffith who had built the house around 1590. Anne particularly loved Burton Agnes, and on her deathbed, according to the story, she asked that her head be cut off after she died and kept inside the house. Several subsequent owners of the house apparently disobeyed her request and removed the skull for burial, whereupon it would begin to scream. The fact that "Awd Nance"—as she was known to the Yorkshire locals—was frequently seen walking through the house was taken as an indication of her sense of insecurity about the resting place of her skull. Around 1900, the occupant of Burton Agnes Hall had the skull sealed into one of the walls to

Above left: another skull that refuses to be buried is this one at Chilton Cantelo, Somerset. It once belonged to one Theophilus Broome who, on his death in 1670, asked that it be kept in the farmhouse where it can be seen today. In the past, attempts to bury it have been followed by "horrid noises, portentive of sad displeasure," according to the inscription on Theophilus Broome's tombstone.

Above: Wardley Hall in Leicestershire houses the skull of Father Ambrose, a Catholic priest who was executed for treason in 1641.

81

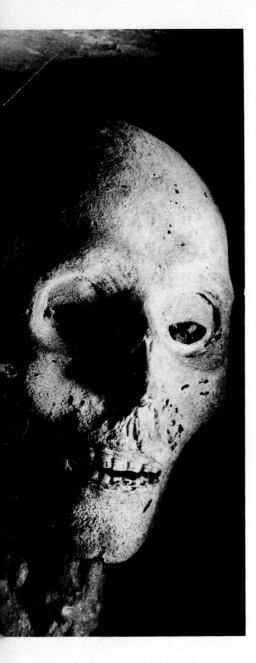

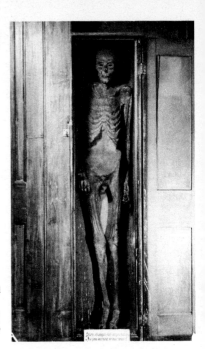

This rather grim reminder of the body's transitory life used to stand in a glass-fronted coffin in the vestibule of St. James's Church in the City of London. Familiarly called Old Jimmy, he may have been one of the City's early Lord Mayors. During World War II's Blitz, a bomb fell through the roof, struck the edge of the coffin, and landed, unexploded, in the vaults. After that unsettling event, Old Jimmy's ghost became active. It was occasionally seen in the nave, and it was believed to be responsible for the movement of objects and peculiar noises. The epitaph at his feet reads: "Stop stranger, stop as you pass by. As you are now, so once was I. As I am now, you soon will be, so pray prepare to follow me."

prevent its being removed. Since then Awd Nance has appeared infrequently.

At Wardley Hall, near Manchester, the resident skull is supposed to be that of a Catholic priest executed for treason in 1641. After being displayed on a Manchester church tower as a sinister warning to sympathizers, the priest's head was secretly removed and taken to Wardley Hall, the home of a Catholic family. For many years the skull was kept on view at the head of the staircase. Occasional attempts to remove it for burial brought repercussions in the form of violent storms and other disturbances. Once it was thrown into a pond but, in the words of ghost hunter Eric Maple, "managed to find its way back to the Hall again."

The folklore surrounding family skulls is full of such bizarre images. The best-known of them all, the Bettiscombe Manor Skull, was once buried nine feet deep in the earth by an owner who wanted to be rid of it. The owner was appalled on the following day to discover that the skull had worked its way to the surface, and was lying there apparently waiting to return home.

The Bettiscombe skull case is a classic example of the confusion and distortion that go into making a ghost legend. One version says that the skull is that of a black slave brought to Bettiscombe, Dorset, in the 18th century. In 1685 the owner of the manor, Azariah Pinney, had been exiled for political reasons and sent to the West Indies. The Pinneys prospered in the New World, and Azariah's grandson, John Frederick, eventually returned to Bettiscombe, bringing with him a black slave as his manservant. Pinney seems to have treated his slave well, and when the man asked that on his death his body be returned to Africa for burial, the master gave his promise.

After the black man's death, however, Pinney broke his promise, and had the man buried in the village churchyard not far from the manor house. During the course of the following weeks neither Pinney nor his family were able to sleep because of mysterious groans, shrieks, and bumps in the night. Finally the master disinterred the body and brought it back to his own loft. This seemed to satisfy it, for no more noises occurred.

The body remained in the loft for years until at some point—no one seems to know when or how—it disappeared. Except for the skull. That remained, minus its jawbone, and has been kept in the house almost continuously ever since. In 1847 a visitor at the house was shown the relic by a housekeeper, who told him: "While this skull is kept, no ghost will invade the premises." This was the first recorded mention of its supernatural qualities.

While investigating the Bettiscombe story in the mid-1960s, Maple found that the local people had plenty of tales to tell about the skull. He learned that on several occasions it had been removed from the Hall, only to bring various disasters on the area: thunderstorms that destroyed crops at harvest time, for example, and the wholesale death of cattle and other livestock. It was even asserted that several owners of Bettiscombe who had removed the skull had died within a year.

One man remembered as a youth hearing the skull "screaming like a trapped rat" in the attic—which somewhat contradicts the idea that it objects only to being removed from the house. Others mentioned peculiar rattling noises coming from the attic, believed to be "them" playing ninepins with the skull. Exactly who "they" were was left to the imagination.

The black slave has lingered in the folk-memory of the villagers 200 years after his death. Tales are told of a screaming black man "kept prisoner in a secret room and fed through a grating." And yet, other versions of the story say that John Pinney treated his slave kindly. Who can say what was the truth? A completely different legend says that the skull is that of a white girl who "long ago"—a favorite phrase of the legend-spinners—was kept prisoner in the house and then murdered.

Neither of these stories is likely to be true, for when the skull was examined by Professor Gilbert Causey of the Royal College of Surgeons, he pronounced it to be much older than anyone had suspected. It was, he said, the skull of a prehistoric woman.

The present owner of Bettiscombe Manor, Michael Pinney, believes it to be the relic of some foundation sacrifice which was placed in the building originally constructed on the site in order to propitiate the gods and bring good fortune. The later story of the black man was somehow grafted onto the original story of this sacrifice.

Although Pinney and his wife claim to regard their strange heirloom merely as a conversation piece, he has so far refused to allow it to be taken out of doors. Both he and his wife were slightly shaken when a visitor who stayed with them during World War II, and who knew the history of the skull, inquired: "Did it sweat blood in 1939, as it did in 1914?"

African or Caucasian, curse or good luck charm, the yellowing relic continues to keep a firm grasp on the imaginations of the Dorset farmers of the neighborhood. If it is, in fact, a reminder of ancient sacrifice, its continuing hold on people's minds for more than 2000 years is scarcely less remarkable than that of the wailing banshee, that "symbolic form . . . stamped on our racial consciousness."

Above: the mummified remains of Jeremy Bentham, founder of the philosophy of Utilitarianism, preserved in a case at the entrance to University College of the University of London. The head is a wax replacement, the original being sufficiently decayed to make it an unsuitable object for display. Something of an eccentric, Bentham wanted his body to be preserved, partly so that it could attend meetings of his followers when they might wish to honor him. His ghost haunts the College.

6

The Poltergeists

To all appearances Shirley Hitchins was an ordinary teenager. She lived with her parents, Mr. and Mrs. Walter Hitchins in one of a row of identical houses that lined Wycliffe Road, a thoroughfare in a working class area of London. Like many of her friends she had left secondary school early to go to work, and she seemed happy enough with the position she found as a salesgirl in a London department store. Then in 1956, a few months after her 15th birthday, Shirley ceased to be ordinary.

Her troubles started one morning when she woke up to find a shiny new key lying on her bedspread. She had never seen it before,

The Drummer of Tedworth, a 17th-century English poltergeist, and one of the early subjects of psychical research, is given visual form in this drawing by George Cruikshank. In reality, no phantom accompanied the Tedworth phenomena—and this is true in the majority of poltergeist cases. Most psychical researchers would probably agree that poltergeist effects—noises, flying objects, and levitations to name some of the commonest—are different in kind from apparitions, and are probably caused by psychic energy from one of the poltergeist victims.

"Her stiff body rose six inches into the air without any support whatever"

Below: one of the various attempts to free Shirley Hitchings from the poltergeist that plagued her for a month was an exorcism held by a medium, Harry Hanks, a friend of her family. After going into trance, Mr. Hanks made contact with a spirit, and eventually received the assurance that the poltergeist would trouble Shirley (right of fireplace) no longer.

Below right: Shirley holds a boot that was the focus of some poltergeist activity during the seance.

her parents knew nothing about it, and it did not fit any of the doors in her home. During the following nights her bedclothes were brusquely yanked from her as she lay asleep, and thunderous knockings sounded on her bedroom walls. During the day such knockings were accompanied by tappings and scratchings in other parts of the house, and heavy pieces of furniture moved mysteriously around the rooms.

Within a few days the girl was haggard through lack of sleep, and arranged to stay a night with neighbor Mrs. Lily Love in an attempt to get some rest, away from it all. "It" followed her. An alarm clock and some china ornaments were shuffled around a shelf in Mrs. Love's house by an invisible agency, a poker was hurled across a room, and Shirley's wristwatch was pulled from her arm and thrown to the floor.

After this her father, a London Transport motorman, decided to sit up one night to see exactly what went on. He was accompanied by his brother. Shirley went to bed in her mother's room. All was quiet for a while, and then a resonant tapping began to shake the bed in which she lay. She was still wide awake, lying with her hands outside the covers. After a while she called to her father and uncle to say that the bedclothes were moving. The two men grabbed the bedclothes and found they were being tugged with considerable force toward the foot of the bed. As they struggled with the invisible force, they and Shirley's mother saw the girl suddenly go rigid. To their astonishment her stiff body rose six inches into the air without any support whatever.

Fighting back their fear, the Hitchins brothers lifted the floating body clear of the bed. Shirley, who had seemed dazed at the time, later said that she had felt a tremendous pressure in

the small of her back, lifting her up. The levitation occurred only once and seemed to mark the peak of the strange events, for the following day the disturbances reverted to the form of rapping noises. These went with the girl everywhere, even onto the bus that took her to work. At the store her co-workers persuaded her to see the store doctor. Skeptical at first, the doctor was finally persuaded that "something was going on" when the knockings began in his own consulting room. He was still puzzling over the mystery when, almost a month to the day after the first mysterious appearance of the key, all the phenomena abated, and then ceased for good.

Today, some 20 years later, it is impossible to judge the happenings in Wycliffe Road with total objectivity, for we have only the contemporary newspaper stories and reporters' interviews with witnesses as evidence. From these, however, we can infer that Shirley Hitchins, her parents, Mrs. Love and her family, and the doctor who examined the girl were all rational down-to-earth people, none of whom had ever previously experienced any form of psychic phenomena.

It seems probable that the Shirley Hitchins case was a genuine example of poltergeist phenomena. The German word poltergeist, meaning a "noisy spirit," is today commonly used by psychic investigators to describe certain apparently supernormal physical effects—whether or not the investigator believes that they are caused by a spirit.

In his book *Can We Explain the Poltergeist?*, Dr. A. R. G. Owen clearly defines the term. It is, he says, the occurrence of one or both of the following taking place in an apparently spontaneous, often sporadic way: (a) production of noises, such as tappings, sawings, bumpings; (b) movement of objects by no known physical means.

These two kinds of phenomena include a host of distinct effects. The noises, for example, may be impersonal in character, such as the rappings that followed Shirley Hitchins around, or they may suggest a human or superhuman agent. The movement of objects may take many forms: pictures may fall from the wall, vases fly across the room, heavy pieces of furniture be moved. On rare occasions, poltergeist activity may involve levitation, like that experienced by Shirley Hitchins.

The poltergeist has a long history. One of the earliest recorded cases took place in the German town of Bingen-am-Rhein in A.D. 355. Stones whizzed through the air, apparently of their own volition; sleepers were tossed out of their beds; and banging and crashing noises echoed in the streets. Since then many other cases have been reported in other parts of the world.

In a book entitled *The Story of the Poltergeist*, the late psychical researcher Hereward Carrington listed 375 cases of alleged poltergeist activity, from the Bingen-am-Rhein case to one in 1949, a few years before the book was published. After analyzing the cases Carrington concluded that 26 were undoubtedly fraudulent, and 19 were "doubtful." Assuming that all the doubtful cases were fraudulent as well, 330 cases remained "unexplained." In other words, they were apparently caused by some supernatural force.

Carrington admitted that the standard of evidence varied

The Drummer of Tedworth

The magistrate of Tedworth in Wiltshire, England, could not have imagined the consequences when he confiscated the drum belonging to William Drury— an itinerant magician caught in some shady dealings—and told him to leave the district.

That was in March 1662. Hardly had the culprit left Tedworth when the drum began to produce drumming noises itself. It also flew around Magistrate Mompesson's house, seen by several people besides the magistrate. After several sleepless nights, he had the drum broken into pieces. Still the drumming continued. Nor was that all. Shoes flew through the air, and chamber pots were emptied onto beds. Children were levitated. A horse's rear leg was forced into its mouth.

The possibility that the exiled drummer had sneaked back and was causing the trouble was fairly well ruled out when it was discovered that he had been arrested for theft in the city of Gloucester and sent to the colonies. The Reverend Joseph Glanville, chaplain to King Charles II, came to Tedworth to investigate the phenomena. He heard the drumming himself, and collected eyewitness reports from the residents. No natural cause was found for the effects, which stopped exactly one year after they had started.

greatly, and that in many cases it was not high. In fact, such sub-standard evidence, coupled with the proven frauds, has always strengthened the arguments of the skeptics. As early as 1584 Reginald Scot in his *Discoverie of Witchcraft* was writing: "I could recite a great Number of Tales, how Men have even forsaken their Houses, because of apparitions and Noises; and all has been by meer and rank Knavery; and wheresoever you shall hear that there are such rumbling and fearful Noises, be you assured, that it is flat Knavery, performed by some that seem most to complain, and are least suspected . . ."

Scot was a remarkable man who, in an age of superstition, hit out with considerable force against those who believed in witchcraft; but his strong skepticism on the subject of the occult in general seems to have led him to throw the baby out with the bath water. Today most psychic investigators would agree that there have been many instances of genuine poltergeist effects.

One characteristic that most poltergeists have in common is that they generally occur in a household containing an adolescent. It seems possible that the onset of puberty may in some way generate the forces that produce the poltergeist effects.

This factor was certainly present in the case of the Wesley poltergeist. John Wesley, the founder of the Methodist Church, was a boy of 13 when in 1715 strange knocking noises began to be heard in the family's house, Epworth Rectory, in Lincolnshire, England. The Wesleys were a large family. Besides John there were 18 other children including Molly, aged 20; Hetty, 19; Nancy, 15; Patty, 10; and Kezzy, 7. In a letter to her eldest son Samuel, Mrs. Wesley described the beginning of the events: "On the first of December our maid heard, at the door of the dining room, several dismal groans, like a person in extremes, at the point of death." When the maid looked behind the door she found no one there.

The following day various raps were heard, and on the third day Molly heard the rustle of a silken gown passing quite close to her. The same evening something began to knock on the dining table, and footsteps were heard on the stairs. As the days passed other noises were added: the sound of a cradle rocking; another like the turning of a windmill; another like a carpenter planing wood. The poltergeist frequently interrupted family prayers.

Gradually the Wesleys became accustomed to the disturbances, and even jocularly nicknamed the unseen presence "Old Jeffrey." In the record he kept of the events, John Wesley wrote: "Kezzy desired no better diversion than to pursue Old Jeffrey from room to room."

Suddenly, after a visit of two months, Old Jeffrey left the Wesleys, and the Rectory at Epworth has been quiet ever since.

The Wesley poltergeist attracted the attention of no less a scientist than Joseph Priestley, a Fellow of the Royal Society for the Advancement of Science, and the discoverer of oxygen. Priestley mulled over the facts of the Wesley case, and in 1784 reported his findings in the *Arminian Magazine*. His article showed that he suspected Hetty Wesley of some unconscious part in the phenomena. It was significant, said Priestley, that "the disturbances were centered around Hetty's bed, and were marked by Hetty's trembling in her sleep."

Above: Nandor Fodor, modern psychoanalyst who made a deep study of psychic phenomena, including poltergeists. Among his work is a detailed analysis of the "Bell Witch"—a poltergeist that tormented a Tennessee family in the early part of the 19th century.

The Wesley case was typical of most poltergeists in that it harmed no one. The Wesleys were also fortunate in that Old Jeffrey confined itself to noises. Many poltergeists have a destructive streak, and hurl crockery about with reckless abandon. Oddly, though, these flying objects rarely strike anyone, and when they do their impact is slight—even when they appear to travel at great speed. Occasionally poltergeist activity takes the form of showers of stones—or even coins, or shoes.

Although poltergeists rarely hurt anyone, there is one striking exception to the rule. This was the notorious "Bell Witch," a malevolent force that tormented the Bell family of Robertson County, Tennessee, for nearly four years. It apparently caused the death of the father, John Bell. The word "poltergeist" was not widely known in the United States in 1817 when the phenomena first occurred. Neither the family nor their neighbors knew what to call the thing that plagued them. The birth of Spiritualism was 30 years in the future, and in any case, once the thing began to talk, it asserted that it was not the spirit of someone who had died, but "a spirit from everywhere." Once it called itself a witch, and that was the term that stuck.

John Bell was a prosperous farmer, well-liked and respected by his neighbors, who lived with his wife Luce and his nine children in a large farmhouse surrounded by outbuildings and slave quarters. At the time of the first outbreak Bell's daughter Betsy, who figured prominently in the case, was a robust,

Below left: the curé of the village of Cideville and his housekeeper, beset with flying furniture and levitating pets—an illustration for a famous 19th-century poltergeist case. The curé had annoyed a local white witch. According to local opinion, the witch got his revenge through a stooge, a peasant named Thorel. The poltergeist activity—which Thorel took the credit, or blame, for—centered on two teenage pupils in the curé's house. When the boys were finally sent to their homes, the activity continued briefly in the home of the younger boy.

Below: this French picture is of a poltergeist. The newspaper *Samedi Soir* sent a photographer to the home of a family named Costa near the French-Italian border, which was the scene of poltergeist activity. The photographer set up his camera in the kitchen, and after an hour-and-a-half wait, he snapped these objects in flight.

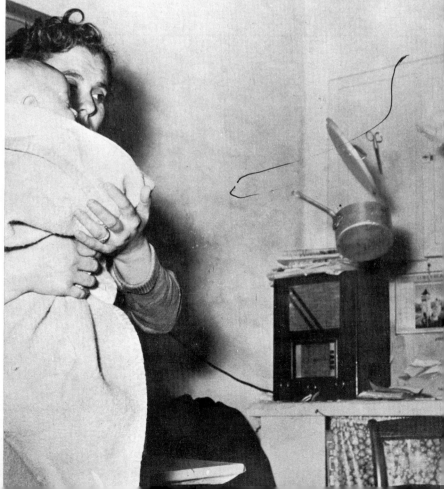

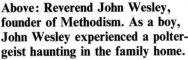
Above: Reverend John Wesley, founder of Methodism. As a boy, John Wesley experienced a poltergeist haunting in the family home.

Above right: Epworth Rectory, the Wesley home in Lincolnshire. The poltergeist produced a variety of noises—knockings, groanings, footsteps, and a curious sound like the winding up of a jack were among its effects. Several members of the Wesley household claimed to have seen a phantom during the two-month haunting. On two occasions they saw what looked like a badger; and a servant once saw something like a white rabbit. Emily Wesley, one of the sisters, believed witchcraft was at the bottom of the Epworth haunting.

apparently contented girl of 12. Richard Williams Bell, who later wrote an account of the disturbances entitled *Our Family Trouble*, was a boy of six.

The disturbances began with knockings and scrapings that seemed to come from the outside of the walls and windows of the house. Later the sounds entered the house, taking the form of gnawing noises on bedposts, scratchings on the floorboards, and flappings on the ceiling. Gradually the noise increased until at times it seemed to shake the house. The Witch continually added new sounds to its repertoire: chairs being overturned, stones raining on the roof, heavy chains being dragged across the floor. According to Richard Williams' book the noises bothered Betsy more than the other members of the family.

It began to show physical strength. Richard Williams Bell was awakened one night by something pulling at his hair. "Immediately Joel [one of the children] yelled out in great fright, and next Elizabeth [Betsy] was screaming in her room, and after that something was continually pulling at her hair after she retired to bed."

Up to this point the family had kept their curious troubles to themselves, but now they decided to ask the advice of a friend and neighbor, James Johnson. Johnson listened attentively to the noises, and concluded that some intelligence lay behind them. He performed a simple exorcism, which helped for a while.

When the Witch returned it did so with renewed vigor, and concentrated on Betsy to such an extent that her parents became seriously worried. It slapped her face, leaving crimson patches on her cheeks, and it pulled her hair with such force that she screamed in agony.

By this time Johnson was convinced that whatever the thing was, it could understand human language and ought to be capable of communication. He advised John Bell to call in more

neighbors to form an investigating committee. Unfortunately, the committee seems to have done more harm than good. The members, fascinated by the effects and presumably safe enough themselves, invited it to "rap on the wall, smack its mouth, etc., and in this way," wrote Richard Williams, "the phenomena were gradually developed."

The Witch began to throw sticks and stones at the Bell children as they went to and from school. Apparently the children soon became accustomed to this and they developed a game with it. When a stick was thrown at them, they would mark it and throw it back. "Invariably," wrote Richard Williams, "the same sticks would be hurled back at us."

This sort of thing was harmless enough, but the Witch was now becoming more violent. Occasionally it struck people in the face with what felt like a clenched fist. Meanwhile Betsy, who had always been robust, began to suffer fainting fits and shortness of breath, each spell lasting for about half an hour. During these attacks the Witch remained silent, but as soon as the girl had recovered her composure it began to whistle and talk again. Its voice, which had been faint and inarticulate at first, gradually developed to a low but distinct whisper. Because the talking never occurred while Betsy was suffering a seizure, someone

Above: the stairway at Epworth— one of the parts of the house favored by the poltergeist, "Old Jeffrey," whose footsteps could be heard going up and down the stairs.

Right: an illustration from a Victorian story about a family troubled by a poltergeist. Poltergeists seldom cause physical harm, but they can certainly turn a house upside down. The late psychical researcher Harry Price believed that poltergeists are spirits of some kind, but many modern researchers would tend to attribute the effects to some force emanating from living persons on the premises.

Right: a re-creation of an event in the bewildering, electrically charged life of Adolphine Benoit, a French servant girl. She had been rocking a child in a cradle when suddenly the locked wardrobe doors opened, linen was thrown around the room, and a cloak lying on a bed wrapped itself around the cradle so tightly that it was difficult to remove. After this incident, the girl found herself the target for all sorts of objects. Baskets of bread fell onto her head; bits of meat and her mistress' earrings mysteriously found their way into her pockets; a large sack fell over her, covering her completely. Once, when she went into the stables, the horses' harness jumped on her, and she had to be rescued.
A priest who tried to exorcise her was shaken, and his glasses broken by the unseen force. When her employers finally sent the girl home she ceased to be troubled; but the phenomena recurred in the employers' house, centering on an infant son. Another exorcism banished the spirit.

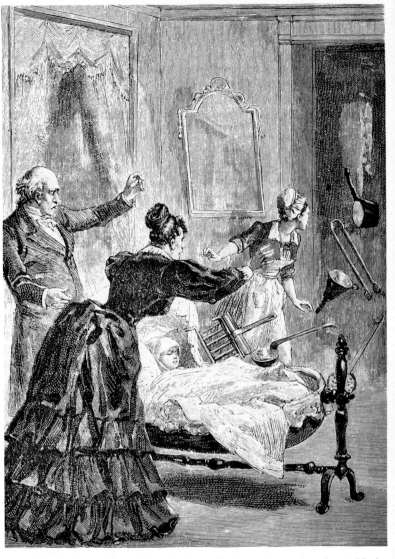

suggested that she might be producing the voice herself, by ventriloquism. A doctor "placed his hand over Betsy's mouth and soon satisfied himself that she was in no way connected with these sounds."

The Witch's first utterances tended to be of a pious nature. It showed an astonishing ability to reproduce, word for word, the Sunday sermons of the two local parsons, even imitating their voices. In a commentary on the case, included in *The Story of the Poltergeist*, psychoanalyst Nandor Fodor observes that the Witch "would have made a grand 'spirit communicator' if it had been imbued with mediumistic ideas." After its pious phase, however, the Witch began uttering obscenities—very distressing to a Bible Belt family. It also declared its hatred for "old Jack Bell" and said it would torment him for all his life.

From that time onward the farmer began to decline. He complained of stiffness in his mouth and of something punching either side of his jaw. His tongue became so swollen that he could neither eat nor speak. These attacks sometimes lasted as long as 15 hours. Then he developed a nervous tic in his cheek. It seemed to spread to the rest of his body so that eventually he was permanently bedridden, twitching in a kind of constant delirium.

The Witch seemed to have mixed feelings toward the rest of the family. The mother, whom Betsy adored, was showered with presents of fruit and nuts which appeared from nowhere. Joel, Richard, and Drewry were frequently thrashed by the Witch, but never seriously hurt. As for Betsy herself, after her fainting spells ceased she seemed to be left in peace—at least physically. But the Witch began persecuting the girl emotionally. She had already become engaged in her early teens to a neighbor, Joshua Gardner. The Witch relentlessly sought to break up the engagement, whispering into the girl's ear, "Please, Betsy Bell, don't have Joshua Gardner, please, Betsy Bell, don't marry Joshua Gardner," and adding that if she married the boy she would never know a moment's peace. Eventually it succeeded in breaking up the relationship.

In the autumn of 1820 John Bell managed to rouse himself from his bed and go about the farm business. But the Witch was not about to allow this. Richard Williams recalled how his father staggered suddenly, as if stunned by a heavy blow to the head, and slumped pathetically onto a log by the side of the road while "his face commenced jerking with fearful contortions." The father's shoes would fly off as fast as the boy could put them on. All the while "the reviling sound of derisive songs" and "demoniac shrieks" rang around them. Finally the shrieks faded away, the contortions ceased, and the boy saw tears running down his father's quivering cheeks.

Defeated, John Bell returned to his bed. On December 19, 1820, he was discovered in a deep stupor and could not be roused. His son John Jr. went to the medicine cabinet, but instead of Bell's prescribed medicine found a "smoky looking vial, which was about one-third full of dark colored liquid."

The doctor was sent for, but when he arrived the Witch was heard crowing: "It's useless for you to try and relieve old Jack— I have got him this time; he will never get up from that bed

Above: Angelique Cottin, a French girl who, at the age of 14, developed a kind of electrical force. It first manifested one evening while she was weaving. The loom began to jerk. The movement would cease when she backed off, and resume when she approached. People standing near her would feel shocks; anything touching her apron would fly off. The effects diminished if she stood on a carpet, and stopped in three months. Left: servants in a house in St. Quentin, France, recoiling from one of the poltergeist effects that troubled the house in 1849. The windows were struck by invisible projectiles that left holes but did not crack the glass. When one of the servants was fired, the poltergeist phenomena ceased.

Voodoo Teddy Bear

When 22-year-old Linda de Winter moved into her own apartment in southwest London, one of the possessions she dug out of storage and brought with her was a cuddly old teddy bear, a favorite toy of her childhood. It looked just like any other well-worn teddy.

The difference was that after being around for a few days this teddy bear began to breathe. "It was horrible," said Linda. "The breathing was slow and rhythmical, but rasping . . ." Her roommate Susan Thackeray and some neighbors also heard the breathing from the inanimate stuffed animal. Linda then remembered an incident from her childhood in which the toy had been involved. Her family lived in Ghana at the time, and one of the servants had slit a hole in the teddy's left wrist. "I later discovered that breaking a limb is a voodoo ritual to enable a spirit to enter a body," Linda recollected thoughtfully.

Was an evil spirit inhabiting this harmless-looking toy? Linda and Susan, who were so frightened they couldn't sleep, decided to take no chances. They requested the services of a local clergyman to carry out an exorcism. "I was naturally skeptical at first," the vicar said, "But when I saw the genuine fear of the girls I realized it was not a joke."

again." Bell died the next morning. As his coffin was lowered into the grave, the Witch had a final gloat: its voice could be heard singing a raucous song, "Row me up some brandy, O."

The family doctor tested the potion found in the medicine bottle on a cat, and the cat immediately went into convulsions and died. Instead of analyzing the liquid, the doctor threw it into the fire. No satisfactory medical explanation of John Bell's death was ever given.

After his death the phenomena gradually faded. As his family was sitting down to supper one evening, a kind of smoke bomb burst in the room and a voice announced that it was going but would return in seven years. The return took place as promised, after Betsy had left to marry another man and only Mrs. Bell, Joel, and Richard Williams remained in the house—but consisted only of a brief scuffling and twitching of bedclothes. After that the Witch vanished forever.

Although some of the peripheral aspects of the Bell Witch case may have become distorted with the passing of the years, it seems certain that the principal phenomena did take place. The case is still regarded as worthy of serious study, and it has been explored at length in several works on parapsychology.

The most interesting psychological aspect of the Bell Witch mystery lies in the relationship between Betsy Bell and her father. First of all, let's consider the symptoms experienced by the girl. Dr. Fodor points out that Betsy's fainting fits and dizzy spells—immediately followed by the voice of the Witch—are very similar to the symptoms exhibited by a medium while going into trance. He also notes that the girl was healthy and sexually precocious.

Her father, on the other hand, showed all signs of what a modern psychiatrist would recognize as acute guilt expressed in physical ways: the nervous tic, the inability to eat or speak, and the general withdrawal from the world. Despite some evidence that an unknown person might have administered the poison that finally killed him, the strong possibility remains that he killed himself—goaded beyond endurance by the phantom.

Describing the Bell Witch, Dr. Fodor notes that the entity could not account for itself or its strange powers when asked by the committee of neighbors. It was singularly human in its emotional behavior, playing pranks, imitating people, occasionally showing great solicitude for Luce Bell.

It also loathed John Bell with the most profound loathing.

Dr. Fodor concluded that Betsy Bell suffered from a split personality—that in some mysterious way part of her subconscious mind had taken on a life of its own. This renegade part of Betsy's psyche methodically plagued her father to death.

The psychology of such a split is still a mystery. Only very rarely do cases of multiple personality appear, but when they do, some powerful emotional shock is usually the triggering factor. Drawing on cases of neurosis and psychosis with which he was familiar, Dr. Fodor made a "purely speculative guess" at the origin of the Bell Witch. Noting that the onset of puberty and budding sexuality would tend to be traumatic in the puritanical surroundings in which Betsy grew up, he speculated that in her case the shock might have been aggravated by the awakening of long-suppressed memories. What were these memories? Dr.

Left: Mrs. Katinka Parker of Denver, Colorado, standing in front of her house, which she claims is haunted. Not only does something go bump in the night; something twice pushed her downstairs.

Below: Mrs. Betty Sargent, photographed in 1950 after she and her husband and baby were driven out of their apartment by a poltergeist. The force dragged her out of bed one night, and another time it tried to strangle her. In a less violent mood, it tore her stockings.

Left: Mrs. Vera Stringer of London sweeps up the charred remains of a wastebasket after the annual Eastertide visit of "Larry," a poltergeist, while her son Steven, age 4, watches. The Stringers' poltergeist has a visible form: it manifests as a fluorescent column of vibrating light, and is about the size of a grown man.

Right: the home of Mr. and Mrs. James Herrmann in Seaford, Long Island, the setting of one of the most thoroughly investigated poltergeist cases of modern times.

Below: Mrs. Herrmann points to the cabinet under the kitchen sink where the poltergeist caused some bottles containing ammonia and liquid starch to "blow their tops." Flying glassware and moving furniture—typical poltergeist pranks—were some of the effects that made life rather tempestuous for the Herrmann family back in 1958.

Fodor's theory was, as he put it, "not for the grim and prudish." He thought that in childhood Betsy may have been molested by her father.

The theory may sound far-fetched, but incest is not as uncommon as we tend to assume—particularly in rural communities. Dr. Fodor points to the fact that the first appearance of Bell's severe guilt symptoms coincided with Betsy's puberty. Perhaps Bell's guilt was so extreme that to some extent he cooperated with the Witch in causing his own illness.

As to why the Witch persecuted Betsy, this is comprehensible if we accept the premise that it was part of the girl's own subconscious. If part of Betsy's psyche was determined to kill John Bell, it would at the same time have terrible guilt feelings about this, and would exact some penance from her conscious self. This took the form of blighting her youthful romance. "The sacrifice [of her engagement] came first," says Fodor, "but the murder, mentally, had been envisioned long before."

Had the Bell Witch case occurred in the first part of the 20th century instead of 100 years earlier, we would be in a better position to evaluate it, both psychologically and psychically. Today psychical research is becoming more and more sophisticated. The Parapsychology Laboratory at Duke University, founded by Dr. J. B. Rhine, is perhaps the best equipped psychical research unit in the world. The staff members go to painstaking lengths in examining many paranormal phenomena, including cases of poltergeist activity. Dr. Rhine's assistant, J. Gaither Pratt, described some of the laboratory's methods in his book *Parapsychology*. In one chapter he tells of the Seaford Poltergeist, which troubled a middle-class Long Island family and was investigated by Dr. Pratt and William G. Roll, another psychical researcher, during February and March 1958.

Mr. and Mrs. James M. Herrmann lived with their two children

James, age 12, and Lucille, 13, at their home in Seaford, Nassau County, New York. Over a period of two months, 67 recorded disturbances were investigated not only by the Duke University team but also by the Nassau County Police. The phenomena fell into two categories: the unscrewing of bottle caps followed by the spilling of the bottles' contents; and the moving of furniture and small objects.

Although Dr. Pratt states that no firm conclusion could be reached as to the cause of the Seaford poltergeist, he observes that nothing ever happened when all the family were out of the house, when they were fast asleep, or when the children were both at school. He also notes that the disturbances usually took place nearer to James than to any other member of the family.

Dr. Pratt's account is of interest mainly in showing to what lengths a psychical researcher must go before concluding that an alleged poltergeist is genuine. Between them Dr. Pratt, Roll, and Detective Joseph Tozzi first ruled out the possibility of hoax by one or more members of the family. Observing the tangible evidence of the force—the smashed objects and spilled liquids— they could quickly rule out collective hallucination. Next, they checked the possibility that the disturbances could be caused by high frequency radio waves, vibrations, chemical interference (in the case of the spilled liquids), faulty electrical wiring, drafts, water level alteration in a well near the house, possible underground streams, radio frequencies outside the house, and subsidence of the land under the house. They held a conference at nearby Adelphi College with members of the science departments, and they called in structural, civil, and electrical engineers from the Nassau Society of Engineers. They examined the possibility that takeoffs and landings at nearby Mitchell Air Field might be causing the events, and they checked the house's plumbing installations from top to bottom.

All of their findings were negative. After almost two months on the spot, Dr. Pratt tentatively gave his opinion that they were not dealing with the "kind of impersonal psychical force which perhaps sometime in the future will fall within the scope of physics . . . If the Seaford disturbances were not fraudulent—and no evidence of fraud was found—they clearly make a proper claim upon the interests of parapsychologists." In other words, in his opinion some intelligence lay behind the disturbance.

Dr. Pratt did not overlook the fact that in the Seaford case, as in most poltergeist cases, adolescent children were on the scene. So far as he could tell during his short visit, neither of the Herrmann children had psychological problems. Perhaps no such problem is required; perhaps puberty itself can trigger off poltergeist phenomena as its energies react with other forces.

The existence of other forces can't be completely dismissed, for there have been some poltergeist cases in which no adolescents were involved. This was true in the case of the poltergeist phenomena at Killakee Arts Center in Ireland, which was also haunted by a phantom black cat. Margaret O'Brien, the only person who lived on the premises throughout the entire disturbance period—from the late 1960s to the end of 1970—is a mature and intelligent woman. Furthermore, she was absent from the house on several occasions when phenomena occurred. It's

Pyromaniac Poltergeist

Father Karl Pazelt, a Jesuit priest, came to the aid of a California couple in 1974 when they were troubled by a poltergeist. The couple, who reported their story to the *San Francisco Examiner* anonymously, believed that it was a devil.

The poltergeist pulled the standard prank of throwing shoes, but also plagued them by setting fires. At one point a plastic wastebasket (shown below) caught fire and melted. Frightened for the safety of their two-year-old son as well as for themselves, they asked Father Pazelt to exorcise the malevolent force. In his opinion this was a case of "demonic obsession"—that is, the "devil is not *in* the people, but *around* the people." According to the couple, the devilish spirit made its presence strongly felt during the exorcism rite "by knocking both of us down."

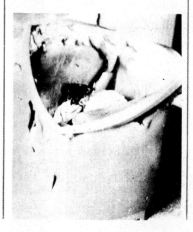

Left: the House of Bewlay, a tobacco shop in Chester, England, the scene of poltergeist activity for several years from 1968 on. Wailing and stamping sounds broke out in the shop, terrifying the staff. Doors opened and shut themselves. A secure picture crashed to the floor, and the screw on which it had hung was found cut in two. Bolts popped out of an oak door. The poltergeist activity would reach its peak in August

Left: an SPR researcher fixes a mechanical vibrator to the wall of a house due to be demolished, to test the theory that poltergeist effects are caused by tremors in the earth, underground tidal movements, or other natural phenomena. The device produced violent vibrations, bringing the house to the verge of collapse, but it did not produce any typical poltergeist effects such as flying furniture.

impossible, therefore, to link the trouble with any one person.

It does seem possible, though, that the Killakee poltergeist may have been goaded into activity—perhaps even created—by some amateur psychic investigators. It's worth remembering that the Bell Witch investigating committee helped to develop the phenomena by urging the presence to "smack its mouth" and make other noises. Old Jeffrey, the Wesley poltergeist, was encouraged to some extent by Kezzy following it from room to room, teasing it. A poltergeist may be an unhuman force, but it often seems capable of reacting to human interference.

After the appearance of a monstrous black cat during the renovation of Killakee House, several other apparitions were reported, though none of them was as vivid as the cat.

Following reports of these strange events in the Irish press, a group of show business personalities from Dublin persuaded Margaret O'Brien to let them try a seance at the house. They arranged letters of the alphabet in a circle on a table and used a glass turned upside down as a pointer that could be controlled by any psychic forces present. The results of the seance were inconclusive—although the lights failed, apparently without cause, at one point during the evening. Within a couple of days of the seance, however, serious disturbances began.

They began sporadically at first with bumps and rappings in the night, and lights being switched on and off. Then some of the artists living in the Center began to suffer sleepless nights, kept awake by the chiming of bells, although there were no bells in the neighborhood. The next stage of activity was more vigorous. Heavy pieces of furniture in locked rooms were found overturned, a stout oak chair was pulled apart joint from joint, and another solid chair was smashed to slivers.

For a few weeks after the chair smashing, peace descended. Then the disturbances began again. This time crockery was flung about and shattered, wide areas of the walls were smeared with glue, and several of the paintings were ripped to shreds.

Toward the end of 1970 the most peculiar of all the incidents occurred. They followed an attempt at exorcism by a Dublin priest.

At this time Mr. and Mrs. O'Brien were still making improvements to the premises, and had not yet installed a refrigerator. Consequently the milkman made use of a natural "icebox" in the form of a cool stream that runs through the grounds. He left the milk bottles standing in its shallow water. One morning when Mrs. O'Brien went to the stream to get a bottle, she found that the foil caps of all the bottles had been removed, though the milk inside was undisturbed. This continued for several days.

At first the O'Briens assumed that birds were pecking off the tops, although no trace of foil was ever found. To stop the nuisance Mr. O'Brien built a four-sided box of heavy stone on the stream bed, covered it with a massive slab of slate, and instructed the milkman to place the bottles in the box and replace the slate lid. Still the caps disappeared.

As if in compensation, though, other kinds of caps began to appear inside the house. In view of the various disturbances, the O'Briens naturally enough made a practice of locking all doors and windows before retiring for the night. Despite this, caps and

The Flying Bicarbonate

The manager and staff of the Co-operative Stores in the English village of Long Wittenham, Berkshire, were not amused in late 1962 when jam jars, cereal boxes, and other normally stationary objects began flying off the shelves and circling overhead. In fact, one salesgirl fainted. To add to the confusion, the invisible prankster switched the lights on and off. For some mysterious reason, the poltergeist concentrated on the bicarbonate of soda, transferring boxes of the substance from the shelf to the window ledge.

After a week of chaos, the local vicar offered his services and exorcised the shop. The ritual proved effective, and groceries stayed put at last. The exhausted manager and staff set about restoring the stock to order. Despite the apparent success of the exorcising ceremony, however, they decided to take precautions with the bicarbonate of soda. They put it under lock and key.

This case is one of many in which possible natural causes, such as earth tremors or an underground river, fail to provide a satisfactory explanation for flying objects. If such natural vibrations were responsible, for example, the bicarbonate of soda would hardly have been given such special attention.

hats began to appear all over the house. There were Derby hats and opera hats, children's knitted hats with woolly pom poms on top, and men's and women's straw sun hats. The pride of the collection was a lady's linen cap with drawstrings which was identified as 19th-century in style, although it appeared new.

This peculiar activity ceased suddenly at the end of 1970, and although occasional knockings and footsteps are still reported, Killakee Arts Center has settled down to a relatively quiet life. It was investigated at the height of its activity, but only in a limited way in the course of preparing a television program on the strange occurrences. It seems a pity that no thorough scientific investigation was conducted at Killakee, for it certainly ranks among the most fascinating poltergeist mysteries.

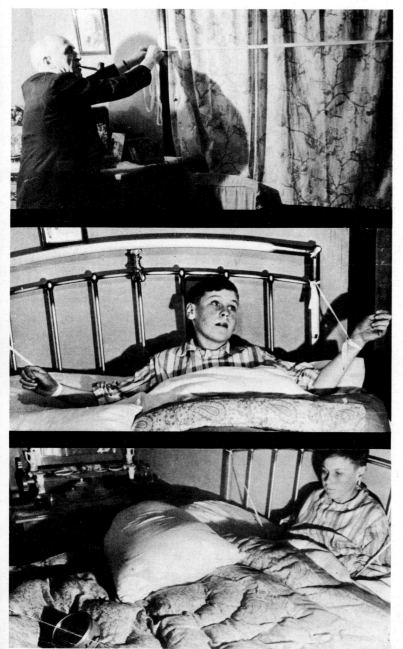

Left: Harry Price seals the windows in Alan's room to make sure no one can enter or leave undetected. Most of the pranks centered on the boy. His face would be slapped, and the bedclothes pulled off at night. Scissors were thrown at him. A more endearing aspect of "Spookey Bill" was that he liked to hear the phonograph, and would leave written requests for music. The family cat, incidentally, appeared oblivious of the poltergeist.

Left: Alan lies in bed with his wrists tied to the bed rails with lengths of tape. He can move each hand about 18 inches, and the bed is near the door so that he can knock to alert those waiting outside as soon as anything happens. Poltergeists, according to Price, tend not to perform when people—other than the victim—are watching, but are not reluctant to give proof of their presence.

Left: an alarm clock lies on the bed—apparently thrown there by the poltergeist. This is one of several effects produced on the night of the investigation. Shortly after this happened, a trinket case from the dressing table was discovered on the bed. The case was not locked, and would have been difficult for the boy to move onto the bed using his feet, assuming that this were possible, without spilling its contents.

7

Enter the Hunters

Just before Christmas in 1323, strange stories began to circulate in and around the town of Alais in southern France. A merchant named Guy de Torno had recently died, and had returned to haunt his widow in the form of a disembodied voice. News of the haunting spread quickly, and within a few days it reached the ears of Pope John XXII in Avignon, 40 miles away. (This was during the Great Schism, when there were two popes, one in Rome and one in Avignon.) The Pope decided to investigate. Fortunately he was able to call on the services of Brother John Goby, Prior of the Benedictine Abbey in that part of France, and reputed to be able

An allegedly haunted 16th-century bed in a museum in West London is tested for supernatural effects by Harry Price (right) and Dr. C. E. M. Joad, formerly head of the Department of Philosophy and Psychology, Birkbeck College, University of London. The test took place on the night of September 15, 1932, and according to Dr. Joad, the only activity was an altercation among three newspaper photographers as to who had exclusive rights to take pictures. This picture was taken automatically, with no one else in the room. Toward morning, the ghost hunters noticed that the bell-cord above the bed was swinging—much to Price's gratification after an uneventful night—but they soon discovered that a railway line ran under the museum, and every time a train passed the cord moved.

Right: amateur ghost hunters flock to the Ferry Boat Inn in England's Fen Country on March 17, the night when the ghost of a girl who hanged herself for unrequited love some 900 years ago is supposed to rise from her gravestone, embedded in the pub's floor, and drift down toward the river. The tradition endures, despite the fact that no one living has ever seen the ghost of the unfortunate girl.

seance. Fortunately Brother John was under no orders to do anything about the ghost, so he could approach the phenomenon with a relatively objective attitude.

A significant aspect of the case was the spirit's discovery of the pyx carried by Brother John. Although the presence of the Host was almost obligatory at such investigations as a protection against any evil spirits that might be present, he had told no one that he was carrying it. Conceivably one of the other monks might have had it. Yet the ghost knew instantly where it was.

Of course the investigation left several questions unanswered. The sighing noises seem less remarkable when one remembers that during the winter that part of France is almost continually swept by the mournful wind called the Mistral. The possibility

Above: a Spiritualist seance as depicted in a turn-of-the-century lithograph. The medium, shown at left, is in a trance, and the materialized spirit looms up beside him. While most present-day ghost hunters regard neither apparitions nor poltergeists as spirits of the dead, some do believe spirits are behind these effects, and try to make contact with them. They may employ a medium to discover the reason for the haunting and help to set the spirit free of its haunt.

that the widow could have created the voice by ventriloquism, consciously or unconsciously, is a reasonable theory—especially if she suspected her husband's infidelity and wanted revenge. Conscious trickery seems unlikely, however, for in those days to communicate with spirits was to invite suspicion of witchcraft and death at the stake. This potential risk, and the fact that the widow cooperated willingly with the investigation, suggests that she was innocent of any deliberate fraud. Yet the annals of modern psychical research are full of cases in which the apparent victims of poltergeists and other psychic disturbances have themselves unconsciously caused the phenomena. In 1323, however, such a possibility was inconceivable, whereas spirits of the dead were not only conceivable but also accepted as real.

A weak point of the investigation is that it was concluded quickly. There seems to have been no follow-up to the first encounter with the alleged spirit, nor any private interviews with the servants to get independent verification of the haunting or of the events in the household while the master was alive.

Even so, Brother John's report is remarkable for its lucid and unbiased presentation of the events as experienced by his team of investigators. Certainly many years were to pass before psychic research would surpass the methods of Brother John.

Probably the greatest single stimulus to the development of modern psychical research was the Spiritualist movement. In the late 1840s in the little town of Hydesville, New York, two young girls, Margaret and Kate Fox, began communicating with some unseen presence in their house. The supposed spirit would answer their questions with rapping noises in a simple code. Soon the girls were practicing as mediums to enable other spirits to communicate with the living. Other people discovered that they too had mediumistic talents. Within a few years, invoking spirits had become a pastime for some, and a religion for others.

Soon after its founding, Spiritualism attracted the attention of some of the prominent scientists of the day, who set up various experiments to test the genuineness of such marvels as flying trumpets, disembodied voices, and materialized spirits. Scientific curiosity about seance-room phenomena naturally extended to apparitions and haunting ghosts—phenomena with a long history. Both Oxford and Cambridge universities had a Ghost Society, each group engaged in collecting and sifting accounts of ghosts and other supernatural effects. By the 1880s the need for a more thorough and systematic study of the supernatural had become apparent, and in 1882 some members of the Cambridge society invited other interested persons to join with them in creating the Society for Psychical Research.

Based in London (there is a similar organization in New York), the SPR has from its beginnings explored all kinds of occult phenomena including telepathy, precognition, and ghosts, and has done so with great objectivity. A large part of its work has consisted of gathering evidence of apparitions and hauntings, beginning with the Census of Hallucinations conducted in 1889. This report yielded hundreds of reports of apparitions, which were then scrutinized and evaluated by members of the Society. The SPR has continued over the years to investigate cases of single apparitions and continued hauntings.

Probably the best-known of all ghost hunters was Harry Price. During his 40 years of psychical research up to his death in 1948, this tireless investigator laid many ghost stories to rest, and brought others to front-page prominence. Using ingenious apparatus, some of his own design, he exposed many a fraudulent medium. But he also discovered and publicized the apparently genuine talents of others. He founded the National Laboratory of Psychical Research, now part of the University of London, and he wrote extensively on his ventures into the world of psychic phenomena. Of all of these ventures, the case of Borley Rectory is the most famous—and the most controversial.

A large and particularly dismal 19th-century house in Suffolk, Borley Rectory had been built in the 1860s by the Reverend

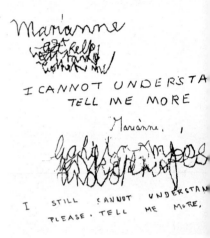

Henry Bull. Like any other self-respecting large and gloomy house, it was haunted, and the most frequently seen phantom was that favorite of English ghost stories, a nun. In addition to the nun, there was the usual spectral coach, complete with horses and coachman. According to legend, the nun had attempted to elope with the coachman, had been caught, and had then been walled up alive in the convent which once stood near the site of the Rectory. By the time Price arrived on the scene in 1929, the ghost of Reverend Bull was also making appearances, dressed in the old gray bed jacket in which he died.

What disturbed the new tenants, Reverend and Mrs. Smith, was not so much the phantoms but the poltergeist activity. Bells kept ringing. For example, the front doorbell rang in the night during a violent storm, and no one was discovered outside. Bell cords would be pulled in empty rooms. Keys were pushed out of locks. Pebbles flew through the air and rolled down the stairs. The Smiths reported the story to a local newspaperman, and on his suggestion, invited Price to investigate.

During his three-day stay with the Smiths, Harry Price examined the house thoroughly, concentrating on the bell system, without finding anything suspicious. He witnessed some of the phenomena himself, saw the nun in the garden, and held a seance in which some presence, claiming to be the spirit of the Reverend Henry Bull, communicated various bits of information by rapping on the back of a mirror in the simple one-rap-for-yes, two-for-no code suggested by Price.

The phenomena continued after Price's visit, and a week later the Smiths moved out of Borley. They were succeeded about a year later by Reverend and Mrs. Foyster, an elderly man with a young and pretty wife. At this point the poltergeist broke into a frenzy. Objects whizzed through the air, doors locked themselves, furniture was overturned. Much of the activity centered on Marianne Foyster. She was occasionally struck, thrown out of her bed, and locked in her room. On one occasion she was half-smothered by a mattress. Messages addressed to her in almost illegible scribbles appeared on the wall. The writer of the messages seemed to be asking for prayers to be said for it.

Reverend Foyster kept a diary of the events, and invited Price to Borley to investigate. Along with two researchers from his laboratory, Price again went to Borley.

Impressed as he was by these new events at Borley, Price soon

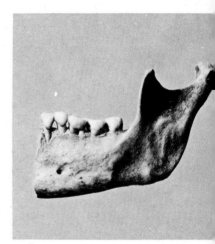

Above: this jawbone, believed to be of a young woman, was dug up in the cellar of Borley, and may have been that of the nun whose spirit haunted the Rectory.

Left: while Harry Price (center right) looks on, the human remains found in the cellar of Borley are reburied in consecrated ground. One student of the case argued that the nun was a Frenchwoman who had eloped to England with her lover. Below: this picture of a flying brick was taken in 1944 during the demolition of Borley after a fire. The photographer only discovered the brick when he developed the picture. The rectory was plagued by many poltergeist disturbances.

began to suspect that many of them were caused by Marianne Foyster. He noted that most of the effects occurred while she was out of sight, or happened to her when she was alone. Whether she caused them unconsciously or by trickery was never proved.

After two years the phenomena stopped, and the Foysters spent a quiet three years in the house before leaving the parish in 1935. The new rector of Borley, apparently wishing to avoid any possible disturbances, decided to live elsewhere. With the house left untenanted, Price could now satisfy his ambition to investigate it thoroughly. He rented the house for a year and advertised in *The Times* of London for volunteers to assist him.

Accompanied by the selected 48 amateur volunteers, Price set out for Borley again. During the next 12 months he conducted an unsatisfactory series of experiments and observations—unsatisfactory because none of the observers except Price were experienced; because all of them, probably including Price, were in an artificially receptive frame of mind; and most especially because little actually happened. Anything that did happen was ascribed to supernatural forces.

After Price and his team left, the Rectory remained empty for a year. In 1939 it burned to the ground in an accidental fire. The following year Price published his book *The Most Haunted House in England*, an account of all the various events at Borley.

Another chapter in the saga of Borley Rectory was added by Dr. Pythian-Adams, a canon of Carlisle Cathedral, who produced a long and scholarly argument asserting that the ghostly activity had in fact been produced by a nun, but not the English

Above: a dog is taken to the site where the nun is said to walk to see if it can detect any clues.
Below: Borley parish church, across the road from the rectory. The figure of the nun has also been seen in the churchyard. While locked and empty, the church occasionally echoes with organ music.

nun of the legend. He said that it had been a French nun named Marie Lairre, who had eloped with her lover to England. There she had been murdered by the lover and buried in the cellar of a house that stood on the site before Borley Rectory was built. Price received the argument enthusiastically, and in his second book on the subject, *The End of Borley Rectory* (1946), he related how excavators in the ruins of Borley found human remains, presumed to be those of the murdered Marie Lairre.

Hailed widely as the most thorough ghost hunter in the world, Price nevertheless had a number of detractors who were critical of his methods and of his love of publicity. After his death in 1948, some of them stepped in to demolish the Borley case. A *Daily Mail* reporter described how he had caught Price in the act of manufacturing phenomena during the 1929 investigations. His story prompted Mrs. Smith, wife of the former rector, to state that she and her husband had never believed the place to be haunted by anything other than rats.

More seriously damaging was a book entitled *The Haunting of Borley Rectory* (1956), written by three SPR members: E. J. Dingwall, K. M. Goldney, and Trevor Hall. The authors meticulously examined—and largely demolished—Price's evidence. They compared Price's notes with his published material and showed how he had suppressed some facts and blown up others to make a better story. They pointed to acoustic data on the Rectory indicating that most of the auditory phenomena could be attributed to natural causes. They leaned heavily on the probable involvement of Marianne Foyster in the poltergeist activity (she was known to have hated the Rectory and wanted to move). By the time the authors had finished scrutinizing all the evidence, Borley's reputation as "the most haunted house in England," and Price's reputation as ghost hunter were largely shattered. Since then, other psychical researchers have tackled the Borley case and formed various opinions about it. Even today, it remains one of the most debated of all ghost stories.

The tarnishing of Price's reputation in the Borley controversy has tended to obscure his valuable technical contributions to modern ghost hunting. He was a skilled engineer and devised various pieces of apparatus and methods of ruling out natural causes in an investigation. An account of how such techniques are used today is given by Peter Underwood, President and Chairman of the British Ghost Club, in his book *Haunted London*.

He recounts that Reverend and Mrs. R. W. Hardy, a Canadian couple on vacation in London during 1966, had paid a visit to the historic Queen's House at Greenwich, built for the wife of King Charles I. While there, Reverend Hardy had taken a photograph of the elegant Tulip staircase. On his return to Canada he had the film developed, and to his amazement saw a shrouded but distinct figure standing on the staircase, its hands clutching the railing.

When the Ghost Club heard of the affair they immediately began a thorough investigation of the story and photograph. The picture was submitted to Kodak, whose experts testified that no manipulation of the actual film could have occurred. Officials at the Queen's House corroborated the Hardys' statement that no one could have been on the staircase, which is closed to the public and roped off from the hall.

Above: checking the temperature at a "cold spot" near the supposed haunt of the nun. One peculiarity of the house was that it was unusually cold—even for a large English house without central heating. One midsummer day, Harry Price found that the temperature inside the house was only 48°F.

Left: Harry Price's ghost-hunting kit. Among the items included in the kit were: movie and still cameras, steel measuring tape, drawing materials, a flashlight, a portable telephone for communicating with an assistant, and first-aid supplies including a flask of brandy in case anyone fainted.

Above: ghost hunter L. Sewell of the 1955 investigation of Borley, in the tunnel that his team discovered. The bricks of which the tunnel is built are of Tudor type. Harry Price believed in the existence of such a tunnel, through which the nun and her lover (in one version of the story) are said to have tried to elope. Discovery of the tunnel indicates that the rectory stood on the site of an older building, perhaps a convent.

Left: an independent psychical researcher, Benson Herbert, in his laboratory. He has made machines to detect psychic energy, the stuff of which ghosts may be made

Arrangements were then made for members of the Society to spend a night in the hall of the Queen's House, joined by the senior museum photographer and two attendants. The official photographer took photographs at intervals throughout the night, all of which had no ghostly figure when developed. At the same time, a movie camera equipped with special filters and infrared film ran continuously, as did a tape recorder. Thermometers were watched to detect any unusual temperature change. Delicate instruments were set to show drafts and vibrations, and the stair rail was coated with petroleum jelly and later checked for fingerprints. Investigators were stationed on the staircase.

Despite all this scientific procedure—plus attempted seances—nothing much came of the night's work, although members of the team reported hearing some sounds that were "never satisfactorily explained." The time factor might be significant, for some haunting apparitions occur only at certain times. The figure in the Hardys' photo may have appeared only in the daytime.

This case is an excellent illustration of a major problem facing any ghost hunter: the ghost often fails to appear. More often than not, the investigator's contribution will consist of discovering a natural cause for the phenomena. In his book *Ghost Hunting*, Andrew Green describes a case of a mysterious "whistling moan" in a forest clearing which campers attributed to a ghost. Near the camp site was a small dip in the ground filled with junk, and just beyond this point the land sloped down into a valley. A professional ghost hunter arriving on the scene first checked the times at which the sound was heard, then determined the wind strength and direction at a local meteorological office. He soon was able to establish that the moaning sound was created by wind blowing up from the valley into the rubbish pit and through a couple of old metal cylinders—the same principle that operates a pipe organ. When the cylinders were turned sideways, across the direction of the wind, the moaning stopped.

Ghostlike noises in old houses often turn out to be no more than creaking timbers, a draft in a closed-off passage, or simply mice. The serious ghost hunter must make a thorough search of the premises, measuring the thickness of walls and tapping them to see if they are hollow, taping doors shut and stringing thread across a passage to determine whether a phantom that walks there might be a living person, and keeping his eyes open for optical illusions and any other peculiar visual or aural effects that might create an impression of ghostly activity.

He must also be a clever and tactful interviewer, collecting various people's accounts of the phenomena and comparing these accounts to see where they agree and differ. In short, he must work as a detective does. Then he must face the possibility that even after he has eliminated all conceivable natural causes, the phantom, or voice, or poltergeist may refuse to come forward. At this point, the investigator must have plenty of patience, returning to the scene or remaining there until the phenomena do occur, or until it seems likely that they have ceased.

Some ghost hunters use a more active approach. Operating on the assumption that if a haunting is genuine it may be caused by a surviving spirit, they attempt to make contact with the spirit. One ghost hunter uses a medium and a tape recorder. The

Ghost Hunter as Ghost

One night in early spring 1948, a young Swedish man awoke to find a white-haired gentleman standing at his bedside. For some reason the young man—whom we'll call Erson—wasn't frightened. The stranger began to talk in a language Erson couldn't understand, but thought must be English. He managed to convey the information that his name was Price.

The mysterious Price began to appear fairly frequently, at times in the morning, and he was seen not only by Erson but also by his wife and daughter. The figure appeared solid and lifelike, but when Erson tried to photograph it, he only got a few shadows on the prints. Price seemed amused by these efforts to photograph him.

Finally Erson acquired enough English to understand that his visitor had studied ghosts and related subjects when alive. It was "Price" who urged Erson to go to a particular hospital in Lund to take treatment for a health problem. While there, Erson told a psychiatrist of his ghostly visitor. The doctor, having heard of the famous English psychical researcher Harry Price, decided to find out from the SPR when he had died. It was March 29, 1948—just about the time that Erson's spectral friend had made his first appearance.

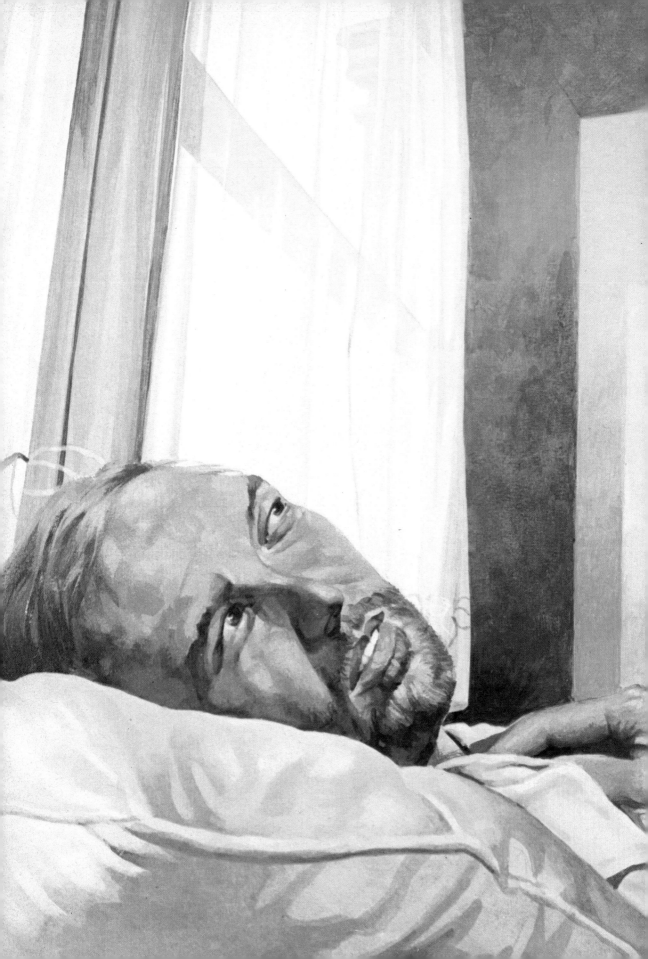

Above: the Haunted Staircase at Tamworth Castle in Staffordshire. Once a convent, it was appropriated by Robert de Marmion, a friend of William the Conqueror, and the nuns evicted. Marmion was struck on the head by the ghost of the founder, Editha, and the stairs still echo to his groans, which have been recorded on tape.

Left: photograph of the staircase at the Queen's House, Greenwich. taken by Reverend R. W. Hardy, showing a shrouded phantom.
Below: Mary Sharman of Leeds, England, with two of her sons. The family was haunted by an apparition and a poltergeist for 12 years.

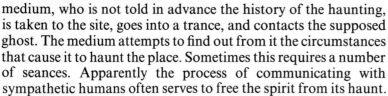

medium, who is not told in advance the history of the haunting, is taken to the site, goes into a trance, and contacts the supposed ghost. The medium attempts to find out from it the circumstances that cause it to haunt the place. Sometimes this requires a number of seances. Apparently the process of communicating with sympathetic humans often serves to free the spirit from its haunt.

Occasionally, a ghost has apparently been driven from its haunt by the rite of exorcism. The main purpose of exorcism has traditionally been to cast out evil, although churchmen today recognize the fact that people who claim to be possessed by a demon are usually mentally ill and in need of psychiatry rather than exorcism. A ritual to exorcise a place troubled by poltergeist activity was provided in the 17th century by Pope Urban VIII, and some clergymen today will perform an exorcism to free a place from a haunting ghost. They admit the possibility—denied by most psychical researchers—that an apparition of a dead person in some way contains or represents the surviving spirit of that person and thus can be dealt with by spiritual force.

One English clergyman who has performed hundreds of exorcisms is the Reverend J. C. Neil-Smith of Hampstead, a fashionable part of London. Among his more bizarre cases was that of the haunted *au pair* girls (young girls, usually foreign, who live with a family as both nursemaid and housemaid). A family living in a large 19th-century mansion had had a run of bad luck with au pair girls. Three girls in succession had taken on the job, only to leave within a few days muttering unintelligible excuses. Finally one of them explained that a ghost had attacked her in the night, and in a mood of mingled amusement and exasperation, the householder called in Reverend Neil-Smith.

"I went up there about midnight one night," said Reverend Neil-Smith, "and entered the bedsitter [combined livingroom-bedroom] in the basement of the house which was used by the au pairs and had always been servants' quarters. After saying a few opening prayers, I saw the figure of a young girl in Victorian costume—three people with me also either saw or felt her presence. I asked her what she wanted, and it turned out that she had been a lesbian and was attacking the au pairs in the night. I prayed that she would find rest, and then exorcised the building. There was no further trouble after that."

Mrs. Mary Sharman of Leeds, Yorkshire, did not find it so easy to get rid of the ghostly phenomena that tormented her and her family for nearly 12 years. The family's ordeal, reported in the *Yorkshire Evening Post* in June 1974, began in 1962 about a year after they had moved into a house in a public housing development. Mary Sharman, who had six young children, was separated from her first husband.

One night she saw the door of the toilet open. A moment later, she said, "a head poked out from the toilet door. Then an elderly woman came out and stood in front of me. She had white hair with tight curls, her head was on one side, one eye was opened and she was giving me a funny sort of smile. Then she shook her stick at me—a white stick."

The following morning Mrs. Sharman told some of the neighbors what she had seen. "That's old Mrs. Napier," they said. Mrs. Napier, who had been totally blind, had lived in the house on her own before the family moved in. She had been found dead in the lavatory.

After the first manifestation of Mrs. Napier came the poltergeist activity. Mary Sharman and her children watched in awe as ornaments moved back and forth on the mantelpiece, and doors opened and shut by themselves. Sometimes they would hear the sound of dragging footsteps on the stairs. The specter of Mrs. Napier would appear occasionally.

"The children's mattresses were lifted up in the night and the blankets thrown in a heap on the floor," Mary Sharman told the *Evening Post*. "I thought I was going insane . . . The children and myself would not go upstairs at night and slept in a front downstairs room together. Every night we barricaded the room door with a sideboard and chairs."

Finally Mrs. Sharman, a Catholic, went to her local church and told the parish priest. The priest performed a "blessing" ceremony—a shortened form of exorcism. He went into each room blessing it and sprinkling holy water.

Despite the blessing ceremony, the disturbances continued. Most of them were typical poltergeist pranks: coats were thrown around the entrance hall during the night; a roll of linoleum was found unrolled in the morning. But one night something frightening happened.

The Haunting of the Toby Jug

The Toby Jug restaurant in the Yorkshire village of Haworth can boast of a specter of some distinction: poet and novelist Emily Brontë (above in a portrait by her brother), a native of the village. According to the restaurant's owner Keith Ackroyd, Emily Brontë's ghost appears every year on December 19, the day she died. He once described for a reporter his first glimpse of the phantom in 1966 after taking over the Toby Jug. "I turned and saw this figure smiling and giggling," he said. "She walked across the room to where the stairs used to be and started to climb up to the bedroom." She was small, wore a crinoline and carried a wicker basket.

The ghost of such a famous writer might be considered an asset, but Ackroyd wanted to have it exorcized. He planned to sell the restaurant and feared that a specter might be regarded as a liability. A curate from Leeds agreed to perform the rite, but was prevented by the Rector of Haworth who wasn't sure it was necessary. Perhaps, like many churchmen today, he takes a wary view of highly publicized exorcisms.

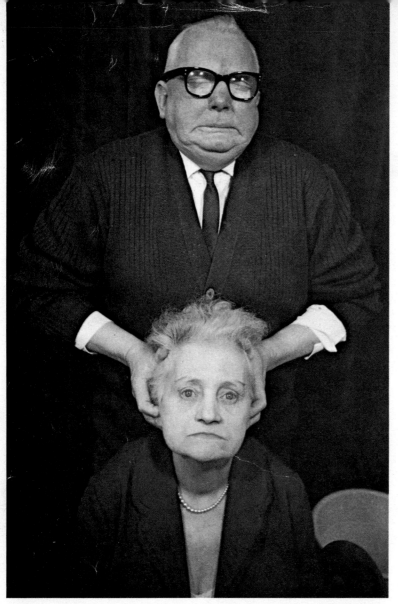

Exorcism, an ancient rite for casting out devils, is frequently used today on disturbed persons who believe they have been possessed by an evil force. It is also occasionally used to free a house or other building of a haunting ghost. Right: Reverend J. C. Neil-Smith of London performing an exorcism.

Left: the English clairvoyant and exorcist Donald Page frees a woman from the spirit believed to be possessing her. His contorted face reflects the struggle taking place.

Below: Page comforts a woman after freeing her house of a ghost that haunted it for 18 years. The apparition, called "Joe," apparently produced poltergeist phenomena as well as appearing from time to time. Page performed the exorcism with Canon John Pearie-Higgins of Southwark Cathedral, London.

The children, who were now sleeping upstairs in one room, had formed the habit of singing themselves to sleep. On this particular evening, Mary Sharman suddenly heard the singing stop abruptly. She and her brothers, who were visiting her, rushed upstairs and into the room. They found her son Michael, aged 12, floating about six feet above his bed while the other children stared at him terrified. Michael's eyes were open, but he was in a state of deep shock. One of Mrs. Sharman's brothers pulled the boy down and tried to comfort him.

Mary Sharman called the police and an ambulance, and Michael was taken to the hospital. The police stayed a while to restore calm, but one of them left after a short time, saying that he couldn't stand the eerie atmosphere any longer.

After being treated for shock, Michael was sent home from the hospital the following morning. Apparently, however, the levitation had left a permanent mark on him. Ever since that night he has spoken with a stammer.

When Mrs. Sharman consulted the family doctor about the disturbances, he contacted some people he knew who had ex-

perience in psychical research. The three investigators spent three nights in the house. Their conclusions are not on record, but by the third morning they had apparently decided that the best course was to move the family elsewhere.

Not surprisingly—considering that poltergeists tend to be associated with people rather than places—the family's troubles went with them. Footsteps continued to be heard and mattresses lifted off the beds. After a while the family began to be haunted by another phantom, that of Mary Sharman's mother, who had recently died. This apparition did not disturb the family, but the poltergeist activity, continuing for years, had its effect on their nerves. At one point Mrs. Sharman called in another priest. He stayed only a few minutes and then left, saying, "This is evil."

Whatever this "evil" thing was, it apparently relinquished its hold on the family after they moved to another home early in 1974. Mrs. Sharman, now remarried, told the *Evening Post* reporter that there had been "no happenings" of a poltergeist type in the new house.

The variety of phenomena experienced by Mary Sharman and her family, and the various approaches they used in trying to deal with those phenomena illustrate the complexity of the ghost problem. If the case had been thoroughly investigated, it is possible that several distinct explanations would have been required to account for its different aspects. The family assumed that the poltergeist activity was caused by the spirit of Mrs. Napier, but few psychical researchers would find this plausible. The presence in the house of several pubescent children would seem a more likely cause for the poltergeist. The fact that the poltergeist followed them to another home, unconnected with Mrs. Napier, further supports this assumption. The other phenomena—the apparitions of Mrs. Napier and of the grandmother—may have been generated in some way by the family themselves. However, it is also possible that the phantom of Mrs. Napier had some objective reality, for she was readily identified by the neighbors from Mary Sharman's description. The terror of the second priest in the presence of something he experienced as "evil" suggests, on the face of it, that some supernatural being had attached itself to the family. Alternatively, it might suggest that suppressed conflicts within the family had generated some negative force to which the priest was hypersensitive. There is also the possibility that the priest's reaction was entirely subjective, created by his own fears.

The ghost hunter must bear many such possibilities in mind when investigating a haunting. If he is skeptical, he will find plenty of evidence to support the assumption that apparitions are all "in the mind," or even that poltergeist effects are caused by earth tremors. Sometimes, however, he may discover a case in which other factors appear to be involved. Similarly, the investigator who is inclined to believe in surviving spirits will find evidence indicating that people occasionally create their own phantoms and poltergeists. Any haunting is a complex phenomenon. Taken together, all the hauntings and apparitions on record constitute one of the most baffling mysteries science has ever attempted to solve.

8

Toward an Explanation

What is really going on when a person sees an apparition? When several people at the same time see the same apparition? When the same apparition is seen again and again in the same place by different people? When an apparition is reflected in a mirror? When photographic film registers an apparition not seen by the person who took the picture? When a person is touched by a hand he cannot touch himself?

These and numerous other questions have been raised again and again in the hundred years or so since serious psychical research got underway, and we are still far from having a satisfactory answer that will cover

Travelers who climbed to the top of the Brocken, highest peak in the Harz Mountains of central Germany, often returned with tales of gigantic specters haunting its peak. The mountain has for centuries been linked with magical rites and villagers believed it was guarded by the ghostly "King of the Brocken." Around the end of the 18th century a climber discovered the true identity of the specter: his own shadow, projected onto the low-hanging clouds by the sun. Atmospheric conditions had thus provided what people expected to see.

122

"How telepathic information is communicated is still a mystery"

all of them. Instead we have several answers, each with certain limitations. We are a lot nearer to understanding the nature of apparitions than we were a century ago, but we are still a long way from understanding them completely.

Before picking up the thorny question of ghosts as possible evidence of life after death, let's consider what happens when we see an apparition of a living person. Evidence gathered in the Census of Hallucinations, taken by the SPR in 1889, indicated that in most cases the person whose apparition appeared was at that time undergoing some crisis, such as a severe illness, an accident, or death. The correlation between the crisis and the apparition in so many cases led the researchers to conclude that the apparition was telepathic. That is, the person undergoing the crisis was thinking about the percipient in such a way as to generate a kind of telepathic message that took the form of a picture of himself.

How telepathic information is communicated is still a mystery, and a telepathic picture is certainly the most mysterious of such communications, particularly when the image appears as a solid,

Right: another impression of the "specter" of the Brocken created by the man standing at lower left with his arms raised. In order for it to appear the sun must be low in the sky and on the opposite side to the clouds. Similar ghostly illusions have been seen on other mountaintops, including those in the north of England.

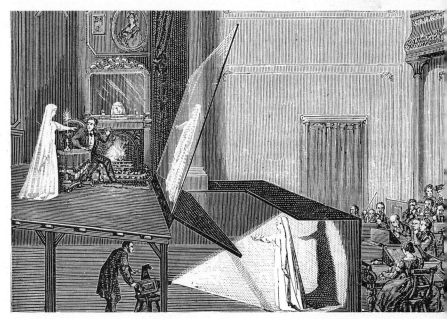

Above: a French playbill of the 19th century advertising the play *The Specters and the Devil's Manor House,* and illustrating some of the theatrical tricks used to produce phantoms in that day.

Above right: Pepper's Ghost, an ingenious theatrical stunt devised by Professor John Henry Pepper in England in 1863. The white phantom onstage at left is not there at all, but appears to be standing in that spot from the point of view of the audience, at right. The actor stands under the stage out of sight of the audience, and his brightly lit reflection, projected onto the angled glass, creates the illusion of a figure standing some distance behind it.

living person. Those of us who have never seen an apparition tend to assume that no one can see anything that is not actually physically present in space. But seeing is much more complex than we normally suppose. We often see things vividly in our dreams, even though we're receiving no visual information through our eyes. While awake, most people can readily see in their mind's eye anything they choose to see, mentally super-imposed on what their eyes are looking at at that moment.

The peculiarities of perception are well illustrated in the case of hypnosis. Experiments have shown that if a highly suggestible person in a hypnotic trance is told that on awakening he will see only the hypnotist—even though there are other people in the room—he will, on awakening, be unable to see those other people until the hypnotist removes the suggestion.

The hypnotist can tell a subject what he will see and what he won't see. Astonishing as such cases may be, they are not quite as remarkable as the case of a person *spontaneously* seeing the image of someone else, as lifelike as if he were there in the flesh. It seems incredible that the agent, or person sending the telepathic hallucination, should be able to achieve at a distance—and in many cases while he is unconscious—what the hypnotist achieves by giving his subject explicit instructions.

The evidence suggests, however, that the agent's mind plays a smaller part in creating the apparition than does the mind of the percipient. This conclusion becomes obvious when we look at details of reported crisis apparitions. Rarely does the figure manifest itself in the agent's form as it is at the moment of crisis—lying on his or her deathbed, for example, or mangled in an auto accident, or falling into a river. Almost always the apparition appears detached from its surroundings at that time. Instead it enters the percipient's surroundings—with which the agent may not even be familiar—and relates to these surroundings just as the agent would if there in the flesh.

In his book *Apparitions,* G. N. M. Tyrrell devotes considerable attention to the ways in which apparitions behave like material

125

persons. For example, he cites cases in which an apparition standing in front of a lamp has cast a shadow. An apparition may also enter a room by apparently opening a door which is later found to be locked. In some cases an apparition has been reflected in a mirror. Apparitions, says Tyrrell, "adapt themselves almost miraculously to the physical conditions of the percipient's surroundings, of which the agent as a rule can know little or nothing. These facts reveal the apparition to be a piece of stage-machinery which the percipient must have a large hand in creating and some of the details for which he must supply—that is to say, an apparition cannot be merely a direct expression of the agent's *idea*; it must be a drama worked out with that idea as its *motif*."

In other words, some part of the agent's mind telepathically transmits an idea of himself to the percipient, and some level of the percipient's mind is then stimulated to produce not merely a recognizable image of the agent, but an image that behaves in a lifelike natural way. It is natural for a real human to be reflected in a mirror; consequently that part of the percipient's mind that helps to create the apparition—Tyrrell calls this the "stage carpenter"—produces a figure that is reflected in a mirror.

Such fidelity to natural laws is not a feature of all apparitions. Tyrrell mentions a case in which an apparition close to a mirror did not have a reflection. Another case collected by the SPR illustrates the unrealistic features of some of these apparitional dramas. One day about a hundred years ago, an English clergyman, Canon Bourne, went out fox hunting with his two daughters. After a time the daughters decided to return home with their coachman while their father continued hunting, but they were delayed for several minutes when a friend rode up to talk to them. "As we were turning to go home," reported Louisa Bourne in an account confirmed by her sister, "we distinctly saw my father, waving his hat to us and signing us to follow him. He was on the side of a small hill, and there was a dip between him and us. My sister, the coachman, and myself all recognized my father, and also the horse [the only white horse in the field that day]. The horse looked so dirty and shaken that the coachman remarked he thought there had been a nasty accident. As my father waved his hat I clearly saw the Lincoln and Bennett [hatter's] mark inside, though from the distance we were apart it ought to have been utterly impossible for me to have seen it . . ."

The girls and the coachman quickly rode toward Canon Bourne, losing sight of him as they rode into the dip in the terrain. When they emerged from the dip and approached the place where he had been, he was nowhere to be seen. After riding around looking for him, they finally went home. Later Canon Bourne—who arrived home shortly after them—told them that he had not even been near the place they had seen him.

One peculiarity of this case, apart from the odd feature of the clarity of the hatter's mark, is that no crisis occurred. Canon Bourne suffered no accident, as his daughters and the coachman feared, nor, apparently, did he even narrowly excape having one —which might have triggered an unconscious telepathic call for help. There is a slim possibility that the hallucination was a subjective one, created by the percipients themselves, who may

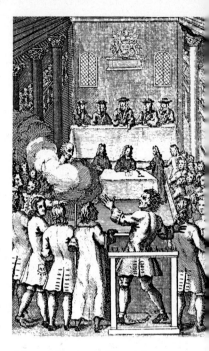

Above: the apparition of a murdered man appears at the trial of the man accused of his murder. None of the live witnesses in this trial, held in London in 1738, had produced sufficient evidence to convict the accused. Suddenly he cried out that he could see the dead man ready to give evidence against him, and he confessed to the crime. On the face of it, this would seem a subjective hallucination caused by guilt, but it could have been telepathic.

Left: the apparition of Mariamne, one of King Herod's wives, confronts the king, who in a jealous rage over her supposed infidelity had her put to death along with several members of her family. When an apparition is of a person who has been dead for some time and is seen by only one person, psychical researchers tend to regard it as a subjective hallucination—particularly when the percipient has a strong reason—guilt in King Herod's case—for seeing it.

Above: the Guildford Ghost shown in a pamphlet about the case published in 1709. Tried and hanged for the murder of his sweetheart, Christopher Slaughterford of the town of Guildford, England, protested his innocence as far as the gallows. His apparition was later seen where he had been imprisoned. In Guildford it appeared to a servant and to a friend "in several dreadful and frightful Shapes, with a Rope about his neck, a flaming torch in one hand a Club in the Other, crying Vengeance, Vengeance." Was this apparition a subjective hallucination on the part of all percipients, or was it a telepathic appeal for justice from beyond the grave?

have had some fear that he might have met with an accident.

The trouble with this hypothesis is that the apparition of Canon Bourne was *collective*—that is, it was seen by more than one person at the same time. According to Tyrrell, "those hallucinations which we have best reason to regard as purely subjective are never collective; so that collectivity would seem to be a sign that the case is in one way or another telepathic."

Collective apparitions present problems. A great many have been reported; 130 had been collected by the SPR by 1943 when Tyrrell published *Apparitions*. It's unlikely that all of these can be dismissed as cases of one percipient verbally persuading others that they see what he sees. On the other hand it also seems unlikely that the agent could convey exactly the same image of himself to several people at the same time. (We are still assuming that the apparition is wholly mental, that it does not exist in the space where it appears to exist.) Tyrrell believes that in collective cases there is a principal percipient who receives the apparition telepathically from the agent, and at the same time telepathically and involuntarily conveys this visual information to the other people present. Of course, not all people are capable of perceiving

apparitions, and so in some cases an apparition may be seen by several people at once while someone else nearby sees nothing.

One of the best-known cases of collective apparitions in the history of psychical research is that of Captain Towns of Sydney, Australia. The incident occurred in the Towns' residence in the late 19th century, about six weeks after Captain Towns died, and was reported to the SPR by Charles Lett, the son-in-law of the deceased man. One evening about nine o'clock, Mrs. Lett entered one of the rooms, along with a Miss Berthon. The gaslight was burning. "They were amazed to see, reflected as it were on the polished surface of the wardrobe, the image of Captain Towns. It was . . . like an ordinary medallion portrait, but lifesize. The face appeared wan and pale . . . and he wore a kind of gray flannel jacket, in which he had been accustomed to sleep. Surprised and half alarmed at what they saw, their first idea was that a portrait had been hung in the room, and that what they saw was its reflection—but there was no picture of the kind. Whilst they were looking and wondering, my wife's sister, Miss Towns, came into the room and before any of the others had time to speak she exclaimed, 'Good gracious! Do you see papa!'"

One of the housemaids passing by was called into the room.

Left: F. W. H. Myers, one of the founders of the SPR and author of the book *Human Personality and its Survival of Bodily Death*. He suggested that a ghost may be "a manifestation of persistent personal energy" that may continue to appear after the person has died.

Right: Edmund Gurney, an SPR founder, authority on hypnotism, and one of the co-authors of *Phantasms of the Living*, published in 1886 two years before he died. Below: Frank Podmore, another early SPR investigator. He also collaborated in the preparation of *Phantasms of the Living*.

Immediately she cried, "Oh Miss! The master!" The Captain's own servant, the butler, and the nurse were also called in and also immediately recognized him. "Finally Mrs. Towns was sent for, and, seeing the apparition, she advanced toward it with her arm extended as if to touch it, and as she passed her hand over the panel of the wardrobe the figure gradually faded away, and never again appeared." Lett adds that he was in the house at the time, but did not hear when he was called and so did not see the apparition himself.

We can account for the collectivity of this apparition with the theory that a principal percipient—either Mrs. Lett or Miss Berthon—passed it along to the others. But the question then remains: Who was the original source of the apparition?

Here we arrive at a central problem facing the skeptical psychical researcher: many apparitions are of people who have been dead for some time. These are called "post-mortem" apparitions. A scientifically inclined researcher, reluctant to assume the existence of life after death, finds it difficult to account for such cases. Myers, Gurney, and Podmore, the authors of *Phantasms of the Living,* came to the conclusion after studying hundreds of cases that an apparition seen up to 12 hours after the person's death could be counted a crisis apparition sent by a living but moribund person. They reasoned that the percipient might not see the apparition at the moment it was transmitted. He might be busy or preoccupied at the exact time the agent sent the message, so that its visualization was delayed until a moment when the percipient's mind was relaxed and more receptive.

In addition, as Lyall Watson has shown in his book *The Romeo Error,* death is not as clear-cut as we commonly assume. If by "death" we mean the complete cessation of biologic activity in the whole body, its exact moment of occurrence is impossible to pinpoint, for many bodily processes continue after the heart has stopped. Conceivably, that part of the brain that sends telepathic impulses might continue to function for some time after a person is pronounced clinically dead.

Thus we do not have to believe in life after death in order to account for an apparition of a person who has been dead for several hours. Deferred telepathy might explain it—or temporarily continuing brain activity. Still we are left with a great many apparitions of people who have been dead for days, weeks —as in the case of Captains Towns—and even years. Some of these can be explained as subjective hallucinations. In other cases, however, the person seen is not known to the percipient but is later identified as an actual person. In such cases it is virtually impossible to claim that the percipient created the image all by himself with no external stimulus. The following case is a dramatic example of a post-mortem apparition of a person unknown to the percipient.

In 1964 in a Detroit automobile factory a motor fitter suddenly lurched out of the path of a giant body press, which had been accidentally activated during the lunch hour. Shaken but uninjured, the man told his co-workers that he had been thrust out of the way by a tall black man with a scarred face, dressed in grease-stained denims. He had never seen the man before, but some of the older workers recognized the description. In 1944 a

The Identifying Mark

Mr. F. G., a traveling salesman from Boston, had returned to his hotel room one afternoon. As he sat working he suddenly became aware of someone in the room. Glancing up he was astounded to see his sister, who had died nine years before. "I sprang forward in delight, calling her by name," he said, "and as I did so, the apparition instantly vanished . . . I was near enough to touch her, had it been a physical possibility . . . She appeared as if alive." Yet there was one noticeable change in her appearance: her right cheek bore a bright red scratch.

Disturbed by this experience, F.G. went to see his parents with the story. When he mentioned the scratch, his mother was overcome with emotion. She revealed that she had made the scratch accidentally while tending to her daughter's body. Two weeks after this, his mother died peacefully.

Psychical researcher F. W. H. Myers pointed out that the figure was not "the corpse with the dull mark on which the mother's regretful thoughts might dwell, but . . . the girl in health and happiness, with the symbolic *red* mark worn simply as a test of identity." He suggested that the vision was sent by the spirit of the girl to induce her brother to go home and see his mother.

Above: a portrait of Dame Elizabeth Hoby, who is said to haunt Bisham Abbey, a Tudor manor. According to local legend, Dame Hoby caused the death of her son. One story says that in a fury over his inability to do his lessons, she boxed his ears so hard that it killed him; another version says that she locked him in a tiny room to finish the work, was called to London by Queen Elizabeth, and returned several days later to find him dead. Her ghost has been seen walking through the house, washing her hands in a bowl of water that floats in front of her. This symbolic act is a bit too picturesque for credibility and suggests that the image may be one of those projected by the percipients.

Above right: Bisham Abbey on the Thames River in Buckinghamshire.

tall black man with a scarred left cheek had been decapitated while working in the same area of the shop floor. He had been pressing out parts for bombers. A subsequent inquiry had revealed that although the dead man was skilled at his job and totally familiar with his machine, long periods of overtime had made him sleepy and incautious.

Telling of his miraculous escape, the motor fitter commented: "The colored guy was real enough to me. He had enormous strength, and just pushed me out of the way like I was a featherweight. I never believed in spooks before, but if this was a spook I take my hat off to him."

One possible explanation is that one of the fitter's older co-workers, seeing him in danger, but perhaps too far away to pull him to safety or even to shout a warning, suddenly had a powerful subconscious image of the dead man which he telepathically transmitted to the endangered man. It is possible to convey the image of another person, although such cases are rare.

We must also consider the physical impact of the push. Hallucinations of touch occasionally accompany a visual hallucination. *Phantasms of the Living* and the *Proceedings* of the SPR include many such cases. For example, one account of an apparition written by the percipient to the person she had seen includes these words:". . . someone touched my shoulder with such force that I immediately turned. You were there as plainly to be seen as if in the body . . ." Oddly, however, there are no cases of the percipient being able to touch the apparition (if we exclude the supposed materializations of Spiritualist seances).

Above: the ruins of Wycoller Hall in Lancashire. It used to be haunted by the specter of a horseman who rode up to its door and dashed up the stairs into a room from which screams and groans issued—a psychic re-creation of the murder of his wife by a 17th-century owner of Wycoller Hall.

Below: Forde Abbey in Somerset. Its Great Hall is haunted by a Cistercian abbot, Thomas Chard, who saw his abbey confiscated by Henry VIII. The abbot's love for the place while he was alive—as well as the trauma of being dispossessed—may account for his continuing presence there.

Either the figure moves just out of reach, or the percipient's hand passes right through it.

Following Tyrrell's theory that apparitions duplicate reality, short of becoming substantial, we can accept the possibility that a spectral hand placed on the percipient's shoulder will be felt by the percipient. This is simply the percipient's subconscious effort to create a realistic apparition.

In the case of the dead man pushing the auto worker out of danger we can't easily use this explanation. What the worker felt was not a mere touch but a strong push. Someone—either the man who died 20 years earlier or a living bystander—exerted psychokinetic force.

Psychokinesis, or PK as it is often called, is the movement of objects by mental energy. The existence of such a force has been tested and proven in laboratory experiments—notably at Dr. J. B. Rhine's Parapsychology Laboratory. Some gamblers have demonstrated the ability to will dice to fall in a certain way. Other tests have shown that some people can mentally influence the growth of plants or the behavior of single-celled organisms. Even animals have demonstrated powers of PK. Unconscious PK exerted by humans would seem to account for many cases of poltergeist activity. The fact that such disturbances usually, though not always, occur in the vicinity of an adolescent girl or boy suggests that there may be a connection between awakening sexual energy and PK.

The PK activity encountered in most poltergeist cases is capricious and sometimes destructive in character. A gentler

Above: illustration for a story in an *Illustrated Police News* of 1872 about a man who encountered a ghost while walking through a park one night. When the specter blocked his path he swung at it with his walking stick but it "passed straight through what ought to have been a head." Yet the insubstantial figure managed to pin him to the ground.

Below: the ghost of Smithfield Market in London is said to hook meat off the butchers' stalls.

kind of PK apparently caused some peculiar events in a bakery in England, described by Andrew Green in *Ghost Hunting*.

The bakery was purchased from a local family who had operated it for several generations. "Shortly after moving in, the wife of the new owner reported that she could 'feel the presence of someone in the bakery.' This phenomenon developed to a stage where doors were seen to open, baking equipment moved and the woman felt 'the entity push past her on numerous occasions.' Both her husband and son began to experience the haunting. Disturbed, they visited the former owners in an attempt to find out more about the ghost, but were assured that the premises were not haunted and never had been during the entire occupation of the original family.

"It was noticed, during the visit, that 'the old man' [one of the family that had formerly run the bakery] had said little during the conversation and 'seemed half asleep most of the time.'"

Green reports that the phenomena continued to disturb the new owners for about two years. "Suddenly, one Tuesday, 'the place seemed different.'" From that time onward there were no more incidents. On that particular Tuesday, the old man had died. The inference seems clear: having retired from the business, the old man had nothing to occupy his mind except thoughts of his former work. He would sit half-dozing, recollecting the activities that he had once performed every day: kneading the dough, cutting and shaping it, putting the loaves onto the trays, and sliding them into the oven. While yet alive, he was a haunting ghost.

Haunting ghosts often seem to be different in kind from apparitions that appear only once, and they are generally considered to be different by psychical researchers. An apparition may be seen in a place unknown to the agent, and almost always appears to a person with whom the agent has some relationship. Often the apparition will seem to communicate with the percipient in some way—by a look, a touch, even speech. By contrast, a haunting ghost almost always seems unaware of the people around it. The place itself—and not any particular human—seems to attract the ghost.

Various theories have been advanced to explain the haunting type of ghost. One of these is the psychometric theory first proposed by Eleanor Sidgwick, an early member of the SPR and the wife of another well-known researcher, Henry Sidgwick. *Psychometry* is the ability shown by certain sensitive persons to receive psychic impressions of a person by touching or holding an object connected in some way with that person. It may be that people who are sensitive in this way can inadvertently psychometrize a building or locality simply by coming into contact with it, so that they will see, hear, or merely sense

Right: the ghost of Hammersmith, London, was actually a shoemaker who wanted to frighten his skeptical apprentices into believing in the afterlife. His graveyard appearances caused panic in the area. One woman died of a heart attack, and a bricklayer in a white smock was fatally shot by an overzealous ghost hunter with a shotgun. **Below:** a cartoon satirizing the credulity of Hammersmith residents.

someone who has been closely associated with it in the past. The apparition would thus be an entirely subjective experience.

One argument against this theory is that almost all dwellings have been inhabited by several, and in some cases, hundreds of people. If a haunting depends on the psychometric abilities of the observer, and not on any action past or present of the persons seen, the observer should be able to see most or all of the people who lived in that place for any length of time. Instead of only seeing the unfortunate Lady L. who committed suicide in 1784, the person would see Lord L., their children their servants, and scores of people who had lived in the house since that time. Occasionally groups of phantoms are seen—processions of chanting monks, spectral armies—but these are the exception to the rule. Most haunting ghosts haunt alone.

The evidence suggests that one's ability to see a phantom or sense a presence depends partly on some lingering aspect of the person seen or sensed. This possibility is supported by the reactions of animals in cases of haunting. Dr. Robert Morris, a psychologist, has reported various investigations of hauntings using animals. One investigator known to Dr. Morris examined a house in Kentucky containing an allegedly haunted room in which a tragedy had occurred. Instead of the usual team of human investigators, he used a dog, cat, rat, and rattlesnake.

The animals were brought into one of the haunted rooms one at a time. "The dog upon being taken about two or three feet into the room immediately snarled at its owner and backed out the door. No amount of cajoling could prevent the dog from struggling to get out and it refused to reenter. The cat was brought into the room carried in the owner's arms. When the cat got a similar distance into the room, it immediately leaped upon the owner's shoulders, dug in, then leaped to the ground, orienting itself toward a chair. It spent several minutes hissing and spitting and staring at the unoccupied chair in a corner of the room until it was finally removed . . ."

The rat showed no reaction to whatever had disturbed the dog and cat, but the rattlesnake "immediately assumed an attack

Left: a typical fabricated ghost of the kind seen in the movies.

Left: an amateur photographer who took a picture of the altar of St. Nicholas Church in Arundel, England discovered a priest's figure on it when the film was developed.

Right: two other priestly ghosts appear in this photo taken in the Basilica in Domremy, France, dedicated to Joan of Arc. This shows Lady Palmer who visited the church in 1929, and was photographed by her companion Miss Townsend. In the developed picture the unseen priests appeared.

posture focusing on the same chair that had been of interest to the cat. After a couple of minutes it slowly moved its head toward a window, then moved back and receded into its alert posture about five minutes later . . ."

The four animals were tested separately in a control room in which no tragedy had occurred. In this room they behaved normally. Apparently, the animals were reacting to some invisible presence in the first room.

What exactly is the lingering aspect of a person capable of being perceived by certain humans and animals? According to Reverend Neil-Smith, it represents the soul of that person. "For the most part," he says, "I believe that the soul of a person who dies a 'natural' death leaves the body for another place. The soul, or spirit, of one who dies violently may not immediately do so; it is bewildered by the sudden transition, and remains earthbound. If you examine cases of haunting which are well authenticated, you generally find that a sudden or unnatural death lies behind the events."

Reverend Neil-Smith thinks that these baffled ghosts tend to develop either a "place reference" or a "person reference." In the first case they haunt a house; in the second case they either possess or consistently appear to a particular person. Reverend Neil-Smith claims to have used exorcism to release many people from possession by a haunting spirit. Most psychical researchers, however, would reserve judgment in such cases on the grounds that there is usually a possible psychiatric explanation for the behavior of the supposedly possessed person. But they would certainly agree with Reverend Neil-Smith's comments on haunting apparitions: " . . . you get the distinct impression that the apparitions are pointless, rather stupid. They wander around, don't say anything in particular, and for the most part don't really frighten anyone. In these cases, I believe, the ghosts are merely trying to call attention to their trapped plight . . . "

Without going so far as to attribute "mind" to the lingering aspect of a person seen, heard, or felt in a haunting, many researchers believe that it consists of some kind of psychic energy generated by the person while still alive. The Oxford philosopher H. H. Price suggested the existence of a "psychic ether" permeating all matter and space. This ether could be impressed with certain mental images. Such an impression would be most likely to occur in traumatic circumstances—violent death, or great emotional suffering. Thus the correlation often noted between unnatural death and subsequent haunting need not be attributed to a trapped soul. The thing trapped in the haunted place would be a kind of recording made on the medium of psychic ether, capable of being perceived in the form of an image, sound, or touch by a sensitive person.

Such a theory has the advantage of bringing the haunting apparition under the same umbrella with the telepathic apparition. If a person is capable of sending a psychic impulse telepathically to a particular person, it seems equally possible that he could project a psychic impulse with no particular receiver in mind, and that that impulse might remain free-floating in the area where the person is at the time he projects the impulse.

Certain cases of hauntings suggest that the generating force

Above: this photo of Isabella Houg of Newark, N.J., taken in 1922, includes an image of her long-dead uncle, unseen when the photograph was taken. Only rarely is a photographed ghost visible to the photographer or to other people present at the time. Apparently, the psychic energy of which phantoms are made varies in degree, and is sometimes capable of being picked up on film, sometimes visible to the eye of a sensitive person, and most often incapable of being perceived at all.

Above: an illustration from "The Ghost Story" shows a lady in a state of suspense, sure to be terrified by the crash that ensues when the cat overturns the plates.

behind this impulse may not necessarily be a traumatic incident. Some phantoms have been identified as images of people who lived apparently happy lives and died natural deaths. In such cases, repetition of their presence over a long period of time may suffice to imprint their image on the psychic ether.

The concept of a psychic ether carrying psychic impressions left by various people alive and dead could lead to a plausible and coherent theory of haunting. If psychic impressions can be left in a place, we would have an explanation for those rare cases in which photographic film picked up an image that people present at the time did not see. In such a case the observers were presumably undersensitive compared to the film. In other cases, in which the phantom is seen but does not show up on film, the observers are presumably hypersensitive.

If we continue on the assumption that a haunting apparition was originally imprinted on the scene by some human agent, we encounter yet another problem: what about those cases in which the haunting includes coach and horses or other nonhuman phantoms? We may without too much trouble imagine the agent unconsciously projecting a picture of himself wearing certain clothes, but it strains credulity to imagine his projecting an image of himself borne in a horse-drawn coach.

At this point one of Tyrrell's suggestions may provide an answer. Tyrrell raises the possiblity that the latent images—what he calls the "idea-pattern"—may sometimes have a collective origin. He cites the case of persistent legends such as the ancient belief in the god Pan, "half human and half goat-like, haunting certain places in the woods and uplands and playing his pipe. The widely spread idea that this happened might conceivably sink into the mid-levels [Tyrrell's term for the parts of the mind that govern perception] of the personalities of a whole community, and there form a telepathic idea-pattern, having a multiple agency. Anyone (suitably sensitive) going to the places which, according to the idea-pattern, Pan was especially supposed to inhabit would then see and hear Pan with the same reality that a person going into a haunted house sees and hears a ghost."

One might extend this idea to suggest that unhuman phantoms such as coaches may have been generated and perpetuated in this way by the percipients themselves.

While some phantoms may be in a sense renewed by the unconscious efforts of the percipients, other phantoms seemingly fade away over a period of time. Andrew Green in *Ghost Hunting* refers to the "ghost of a woman in red shoes, a red gown and a

Left: this illustration from William Gordon Davis' "The Interrupted Ghost Story" is an amusing comment on the effect of state-of-mind on perception. The storyteller has just reached the point where the hero, "transfixed with terror" in a slimy dungeon awaiting some horrible doom, hears an "unearthly yell [ring] through the stilly clearness of the winter's night." At this moment a donkey brays outside the house, causing pandemonium inside it. Such readiness to believe in a ghost will often account for extremely lifelike hallucinations. Yet many apparitions are seen by people in a calm state of mind, totally unprepared to see a ghost; and they often appear so solid and lifelike that they are assumed to be alive.

The Well-Mannered Specter

During the time of the Napoleonic Wars, a German named Wesermann had been trying experimentally to send his apparition to various people. One night he decided to try instead to transmit the image of someone else. A lady who had died five years before was to appear to a Lieutenant N. in a dream at about 10:30 p.m.

As it happened, Lieutenant N. had not yet gone to bed but was visiting a friend, Lieutenant S. The two were chatting, and N. was just about to go to his room when the kitchen door opened and, in the words of S., "a lady entered, very pale . . . about five feet four inches in height, strong and broad in figure, dressed in white, but with a large black kerchief which reached to below the waist. She . . . greeted me with the hand three times in complimentary fashion, turned round to the left toward Herr N., and waved her hand to him three times; after which the figure quietly, and again without any creaking of the door, went out."

The case is interesting because the behavior of the apparition was suited to the circumstances, which were not foreseen by the agent. He had expected N. to be asleep. The apparition behaved like a real person in greeting both men.

black headdress" which was seen during the 18th century in a remote corridor of an English mansion. "Many years passed before the apparition was seen again, and by then . . . it appeared as a female in a pink dress, pink shoes, and a gray headdress. She was not witnessed again until the mid-19th century, when the figure had dwindled down to 'a lady in a white gown and with gray hair.' Just before the last war all that was reported was 'the sound of a woman walking along the corridor and the swish of her dress.' In 1971, shortly before the demolition of the property involved, workmen 'felt a presence in one of the old corridors."

Whether an apparition fades away or remains vivid for centuries, we can usually account for its activities without supposing that they are governed by the surviving spirit of the person it represents. F. W. H. Myers, who devoted considerable effort to the study of the survival question, was careful not to let his wish to believe in survival affect his conclusion. In his book *Human Personality and its Survival of Bodily Death*, he defines a ghost as "*a manifestation of persistent personal energy*, or . . . an indication that some kind of force is being exercised after death in some way connected with a person previously known on earth." He goes on to add that "this force or influence, which after a man's death creates a phantasmal impression of him, may indicate no continuing action on his part, but may be some residue of the force or energy which he generated while yet alive." Myers' hypothesis agrees fundamentally with H. H. Price's concept of mental images being impressed upon a psychic ether.

Yet Myers and other serious psychical researchers have occasionally come across cases that strongly suggest that a postmortem apparition may be more than a remnant of an extinct consciousness. To quote Lyall Watson, "behind every ghost there may be a conscious projector." Watson is not entirely convinced of the likelihood of survival, but in *The Romeo Error* he includes this interesting case relevant to the question:

"In 1921, James Chaffin of North Carolina died, leaving all his property to one of his four sons who himself died intestate a year later. In 1925, the second son was visited by his dead father dressed in a black overcoat, who said 'You will find my will in my overcoat pocket.' When the real coat was examined, a roll of paper was found sewn into the lining with instructions to read the 27th chapter of Genesis in the family Bible. Folded into the relevant pages was a later will than the first one, dividing the property equally between all four sons."

The case of the factory worker saved by the apparent intervention of a person 20 years dead is another piece of evidence in favor of the survival theory. The possiblity that in the moment of his own tragic death the first man left a psychic impression of himself in that place does not explain how this lingering psychic impression could act physically when circumstances demanded it. If we suppose that the endangered man happened to pick up the latent image of the dead man, and that at the same time he subliminally became aware of some danger to himself, without realizing what it was, and that he then converted his subliminal fear into a purely subjective hallucination of an arm pushing him out of the way, we are constructing a rather cumbersome and unlikely explanation. Some people would consider it a more

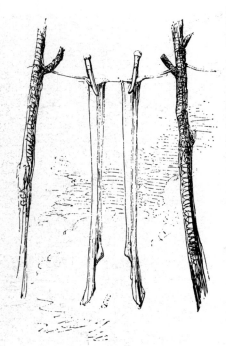

Above: *Ghosts of Stockings* by Cruikshank illustrates the artist's belief that, since spirits always wear clothes, and since theology does not allow for the existence of ghosts of clothes, spirits themselves do not exist. Of course his reasoning was based on a misconception of a ghost's nature.

unlikely explanation than the idea of the dead man's spirit manifesting itself in the form of an image and a psychokinetic force. The possibility remains, of course, that both the image and the force were transmitted by a living worker. Here, as so often, the case is not airtight.

No doubt many more such cases will be collected and analyzed before science achieves a theory that will satisfactorily explain all the ghostly phenomena people experience. Certainly this area of psychical research is one of the most challenging fields of study. Whether or not we ever solve the survival question, we will probably someday in the near future have a better understanding of our own perception and our latent psychic powers, thanks to the efforts of the ghost hunters.

Below: *Apparition*, **a painting by Clairin, conveys the mystery that has always surrounded spectral figures, although few of those reported wear the classic white shroud. Many serious researchers regard apparitions—or ghosts in the more common term—as proved beyond reasonable doubt. Yet much mystery remains as to their exact material and spiritual nature.**